THE
FRONT
GARDEN

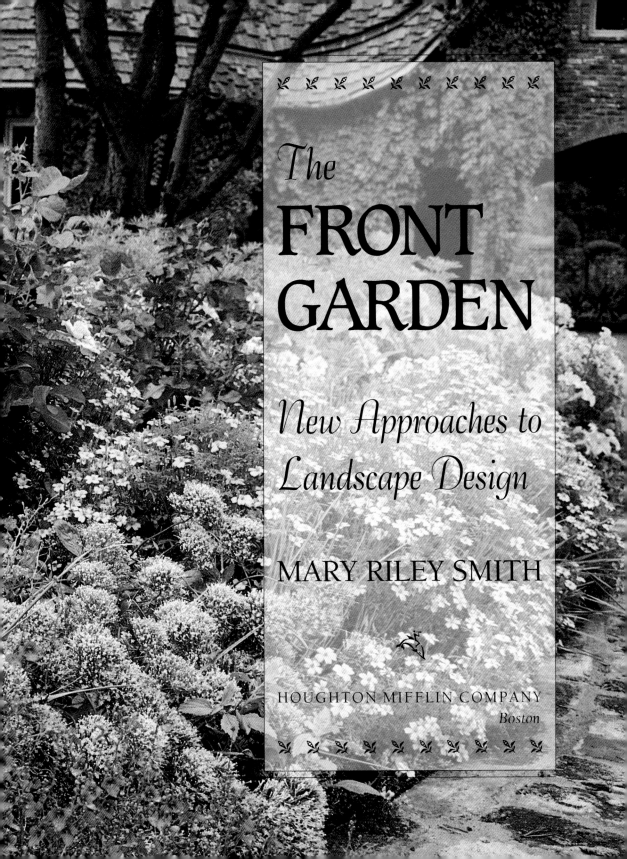

The
FRONT
GARDEN

New Approaches to
Landscape Design

MARY RILEY SMITH

HOUGHTON MIFFLIN COMPANY
Boston

Published in the United States by
Houghton Mifflin Company
222 Berkeley Street
Boston, MA 02116

Visit our Web site:www.houghtonmifflinbooks.com.

The Front Garden
A Packaged Goods Inc. Book

Editor: Anne M. Halpin
Designer: Kathleen Westray
Production Manager: Linda Winters
Managing Editor: Lindsey Crittenden
Photo Editor: Ellie Watson
Photo Researcher: Tonia Smith

Typeset by Dix Type
Color separations by Hong Kong Scanner Craft Co., Ltd.
Printed in Hong Kong

Library of Congress Cataloging-in-Publication Data
Smith, Mary Riley.
    The front garden: new approaches to landscape design / Mary Riley Smith.
p.   cm.
Includes bibliographical references and index.
ISBN 0-618-08342-1
1. Landscape gardening. 2. Gardens — Design. 3. Landscape architecture.
I. Title.
SB473.5366   1991
712'.6—dc20   90-46192   CIP

10 9 8 7 6 5 4 3 2 1

For Mother,
who taught me to love flowers
and gardens

There are few of us who cannot
remember a front yard garden
which seemed to us a very paradise
in childhood.

  Sarah Orne Jewett, *Country Byways*, 1881

CONTENTS

INTRODUCTION

*F*RONT yards are the stepchildren of garden design in America. As the setting for a house, and the daily connection via driveway and entrance paths to the larger world, the front property deserves more attention than it gets. In the current enthusiasm for horticulture, perennial gardens, vegetable gardens, and rock gardens are being designed and planted at a great rate in back yards everywhere. But the front yard, often anonymous and underused, has been left to languish. On many properties the front may be the best, or only, place to have a garden. All sorts of creative designs are possible.

As a garden designer, I find that most front yards are fairly complex arrangements of horticulture and architecture. Hedges, shrubs, trees, flowers, and even vegetables can enhance the architecture and even soften, disguise, or hide a less-than-ideal situation. In a successful front yard, the design of the house and the landscape are integrated to make a welcoming atmosphere.

A late nineteenth-century house and garden in Portsmouth, New Hampshire, is set off by an elegant fence.

To create a well-designed front garden, one must understand how this area functions and how it can work with the architectural framework of the property to accommodate the various activities of daily life—residents and visitors coming and going from the house, cars being parked, garbage collectors and other service people doing their jobs.

The front yard has two somewhat contradictory functions. It serves as both our connection to and our separation from the surrounding community. The driveway, paths, and views into and out of the property create the connection between our individual, personal world and the greater public world. But the front yard is also our privacy buffer between these two worlds. If the front is hedged or fenced from the street, if the house is hidden behind tall trees, our home and front yard are separated from the community to a greater extent than if we have an expanse of lawn from the front porch to the sidewalk. On the other hand, when the whole front yard has been turned into a bright flower garden, we are sharing our private oasis with our neighbors, asking them to stop and admire our flowers and our gardening ability. We are offering our front garden to enliven the street and neighborhood. Whether the front yard should be closed and private or an open display is a philosophic question to be mulled over by homeowners engaged in designing their front yards.

This book explores the potential for interesting and innovative garden design in the front of residential properties. It opens with a look at the history of front garden design, from the dooryard plots of colonial days to the foundation plantings and sweeping lawns of the Victorians to the parklike suburban developments built after World War II. It offers guidelines to help you evaluate your front landscape and choose from among the many options.

Suggestions are given for enclosing the front yard with hedges, hedgerows, or fences to create a private, secluded feeling. If openness suits your needs, there are more interesting solutions than an expanse of green lawn. Landscaping with flowers, ornamental grasses, or native plants; building a Spanish-style courtyard; or planting a romantic orchard are some of the possibilities. You can even install a pool or tennis court out front if your back yard is not suitable.

To demonstrate how these and other ideas can become reality, the book concludes with nine case studies of successfully designed front properties, along with photographs and plans showing how the various elements relate to each other. The nine gardens are of different styles, designed to meet the needs of the homeowners and to deal with particular site conditions. The case studies cover a variety of geographic areas representative of the many climates in the United States. Some of the gardens were designed by professional designers, others were the creation of homeowners. The diverse styles range from a front yard in California turned over entirely to colorful edible plants to an architectural courtyard on a Connecticut hilltop composed of walls and fences. The designers and homeowners were generous with their time, which enabled me to understand and write about their designs and philosophies. I hope all gardeners will be inspired by the imaginative way they approached the challenge of the front landscape. Most of all, I hope the ideas and solutions in this book will lead you to transform your own front yard into a beautiful, personal, and usable space.

The elaborate filigree of a wrought-iron fence and gate creates a substantial entrance. The fence separates the property from the street yet allows visitors a view in.

THE
FRONT
GARDEN

AMERICAN FRONT YARD TRADITIONS

In Greenfield Village, Michigan, a reconstructed Cotswold stone wall is the setting for a cottage garden of old-fashioned flowers, including physostegia, purple coneflower, rudbeckia, and daylilies.

*T*H E front gardens of the earliest American homes were enclosed by fences that were like extensions of the house, arms reaching out protectively to embrace and claim the space in front. Spanish settlers in Florida and California made courtyard entrances by building stucco walls, and the pilgrims in Massachusetts built snug cottage gardens surrounded by rough wood or stone fencing. These first gardens contained edible and medicinal plants and were essential for survival.

The history of American front yards is one of evolution from enclosed, private yards to open, democratic spaces virtually indistinguishable from those on either side. In the last seventy years, foundation plantings, sweeping expanses of lawn, and groups of trees and shrubs have characterized the front yard style.

The word "yard," or *yerd* in middle English, means enclosure, but the meaning has evolved over time to indicate the outdoor space relating to a house, as in front yard and back yard. American houses built after 1860 generally have open front yards. We seem not to want "yerds" or enclosures. Europeans visiting the United States often comment on the lack of separation between properties and the absence of gardens in front yards, especially in suburban areas. The English gardener and writer Vita Sackville-West noted, "Americans must be far more brotherly-hearted than we are, for they do not seem to mind being over-looked. They have no sense of private enclosure."

· The Colonial Dooryard Garden ·

T H E ability to make and keep thriving gardens protected the early settlers from starvation and illness. English and Dutch colonists in the Northeast and Virginia brought seeds for food, medicine, seasonings, and flowers, which they planted in enclosed gardens adjacent to their dwellings, just as they had at home. This essential garden, planted right at the kitchen door, where it could be tended, used, and protected from foraging animals, was the domain of the women. In addition to skill in preparing and storing food, women had to understand the medicinal uses of plants at a time when sickness was prevalent and doctors were scarce.

The earliest dooryard gardens are not documented by drawings or written descriptions. However, garden historians have been able to reconstruct a few seventeenth-century home gardens through archeology and careful reading of colonists' letters and diaries. At the John Whipple House, built about 1640 in Ipswich, Massachusetts, the reconstructed front garden is enclosed by a rough wood fence with a center gate. A path leads straight to the front door, passing between six raised beds built of boards held in place by wooden pegs. Based on thorough research, the restored beds are planted densely with almost a hundred varieties of herbs and vegetables. The House of Seven Gables in Salem, Massachusetts, has a similar garden of raised beds in front of the house. Raised beds have the advantage of good drainage and allow the sun to warm the earth earlier in spring, giving a few weeks' advantage for planting. The distinct and tidy pattern of raised beds gives the gardens visual appeal.

The tradition of cottage gardens in England and America is an enduring one, and the practical arrangements have stayed the same over hundreds of years. Typically, a central path from the door to a gate was bisected by several lateral paths between the planting beds. In very early gardens the paths would have been of tamped earth or stones from the beds. Espaliered fruit trees and shrubs with small fruits, such as currants or blueberries, ranged around the perimeter of the garden. In the center, edible plants were grouped together for easy maintenance, and smaller flowers and herbs lined the paths.

These early gardens were beautiful as well as serviceable. Accounts by Englishman John Josslyn of visits to gardens in and around Boston in 1638 and 1663 mention such familiar bright flowers as marigolds, lunaria, dianthus (pinks), hollyhocks, roses, and fritillaria. Many of these plants were thought to have medicinal properties, so they were both beautiful and functional. The numerous herbs Josslyn saw in the gardens included spearmint, feverfew, coriander, dill, and comfrey. They provided medicine and seasoning as well as flowers. As time passed, and the colonists grew more prosperous and secure, gardens at the front door remained, not as a necessity but as a tradition.

· The Timeless Cottage Garden ·

COTTAGE gardens, like all good designs, function well, are a pleasure to look at, and have become a constant in the garden vocabulary. They blur the boundaries between farm and garden, for they serve as both. Their appeal comes from the old-time values of caring and nurturing, values we all want our homes to embody. The intimate scale and size of a cottage garden suits a modest place, and the variety of flowers and plants makes an endlessly interesting picture.

Cottage gardens were a feature of the

Two views of the swept flower yard at the Tullie Smith House at the Atlanta Historical Society, left and below. The gardens at the simple plantation-style house (circa 1830) are enclosed by a picket fence to keep animals out. The rock-edged beds contain heirloom varieties of annuals, perennials, and herbs. At the seventeenth-century House of the Seven Gables in Salem, Massachusetts, right, raised beds filled with bright flowers and boxwood form the entrance garden. Colonial gardens used raised beds because the soil, warmed by the sun, thawed early, allowing earlier planting.

New England landscape much loved by Alice Morse Earle, who at the turn of the century wrote several books about colonial domestic life in the United States. *Old Time Gardens,* written in 1901, describes the cottage gardens still found in New England villages. "Even where the front yard was but a narrow strip of land before a tiny cottage, it was carefully fenced in, with a gate that was kept rigidly closed and latched. Often the fence around the front yard was the only one on the farm; everywhere else were boundaries of great stone walls; or if there were rail fences, the front yard fence was the only painted one."

Describing the plants, she writes: "The front yard was sacred to the best beloved, or at any rate the most honored, garden flowers of the house mistress, and was preserved by its fences from inroads of cattle." Mrs. Earle catalogs the flowers found in these gardens: daffodils and poet's narcissus, tulips, grape hyacinths, phlox—"the only American native"—Canterbury bells, fritillaria, and lemon lilies (hemerocallis); she devotes several pages to peonies. Of shrubs, Earle mentions that "by inflexible law there must be a Lilac"; she also names viburnums and currants. In explaining the "rightness" of a cottage garden, she notes, "Our old New England houses were suited in color and outline to their front yards as to our landscape."

The American cottage garden never entirely disappeared and is now making a comeback. With renewed interest in old-fashioned flowers, and with authentic restorations of houses and grounds, gardeners are rediscovering the satisfactions of this kind of garden.

· The Eighteenth-Century Pleasure Garden ·

A S the population of the colonies expanded and life became more secure, houses and grounds became a little grander. Modest houses retained their simple dooryard gardens, but as wealth increased some people had the means and interest to plant large, fashionable gardens for enjoyment. Recent excavations at Bacon's Castle in Virginia have revealed the outlines of a large geometric garden dating from 1680, which is now considered the oldest example in the United States of a garden designed for pleasure. Such plantations were built more frequently in the southern colonies, where the economy was based on large-scale agriculture that produced great wealth. Travel was easier by water than by the rough roads, and many of the grand houses faced a river. Often the pleasure garden was located between the house and river, enclosed by a hedge or wall. The popular style of this period was the formal, enclosed Dutch–English garden laid out in geometric patterns, edged by low shrubs such as boxwood. Fanciful topiary shapes made charming accents.

The restored grounds of the William Paca House in Annapolis, Maryland, laid out as a series of gardens strictly enclosed by clipped hedges, exemplify this formal design. Each enclosure contains a geometric garden highlighted by gravel paths, which contrast with the green boxwood edging. Topiary is the focal point in several of the gardens.

The tradition of enclosed gardens at the front of the house continued, in many cases on a grander, more formal scale than in earlier times. A drawing done about 1740 of the governor's mansion at Williamsburg, Virginia, from Arthur A. Shurcliff's *Gardens of the Governor's Palace, Williamsburg,*

shows a large house near the center of the property. Fences and small detached buildings extend forward from the sides of the house, creating, in effect, a front courtyard. A gate and path lead to the front door, and another path bisects the space, making four garden beds. A fence parallel to the front of the house separates the front garden from the back of the house, where a larger fenced garden is laid out with many small geometric beds.

George Washington's home at Mount Vernon, Virginia, is one of the most carefully documented and researched gardens in America. It offers an outstanding example of the entrance arrangement of an eighteenth-century house. Washington made plans for the house and grounds in 1787 and worked for many years after that to realize his ideas. Colonnades connect the main house to a pair of smaller buildings, which face each other across a large lawn surrounded by a circular drive. A curving, U-shaped drive extends out to the road from the turning circle. On both sides of the drive are enclosed gardens; one is the kitchen garden, the other is planted with flowers and espaliered trees. Large woodsy groves of

Two enclosed eighteenth-century gardens: left, in Greenfield Village, Michigan, a country garden with daylilies along the stone wall; above, an enclosed town garden at the Paca House, Annapolis, Maryland, with formal parterres edged with brick and boxwood. A Magnolia grandiflora is the focal point.

trees collected by Washington create areas of shade along the drive and partially conceal the view of the main house and outbuildings.

"The result was a bold and innovative approach to the house. In most estates of the period, the entrance drive stood clearly in the open, but Mount Vernon's drive curves through trees, providing passing views of the wide lawn, called the bowling green, that stretches out before the house," wrote Diane Kostial McGuire in her recent book, *Gardens of America.* The flower and vegetable gardens are more typical of the period, being enclosed by walls and arranged in rectangular beds. According to McGuire, the design of the curving drive with groups of trees spaced along its length anticipates the naturalistic landscape design philosophy that would become popular in America in another fifty years.

· *The Spanish Courtyard* ·

W H I L E English and Dutch gardens were fashionable on the eastern seaboard, in California and to a lesser extent in Florida, Spanish courtyard gardens were the prevailing style. Saint Augustine, Florida, was settled by the Spanish in 1565, the first European settlement in the New World. Descriptions of the town from that time tell of houses and stone-walled gardens with room for fruit trees, herbs, and flowers. Another outpost of the Spanish style was established in California in 1769 when Father Junipero Serra founded a chain of Franciscan missions that eventually ranged from San Diego to San Francisco. In both Florida and California, Spanish settlers introduced a great many crops that have become staples of those states' economies, most notably, of course, citrus fruit.

Despite the differences in weather and topography—Florida is flat and humid, while California is mountainous and dry—the romantic Spanish entrance court, with stucco walls, cool tile floors, and perhaps a fountain, was well suited to the hot climate in both locales. Entrance courts are an important element of Spanish architecture and garden making, as relevant today as they were in the eighteenth century. A court provides a gracious transition from public to private space and creates an intimate, roofless outdoor room for fine-weather living. Spanish-style entrance courts are to Florida and the Southwest what cottage gardens are to the Northeast—a traditional regional style reminiscent of the past.

· *Victorian Eclecticism* ·

EXUBERANCE and eclecticism are the hallmarks of gardens and architecture of the Victorian era. New wealth and technology enabled public botanical gardens to build grand glass conservatories and to fill them with exotic plants from around the world. Even private houses sprouted small conservatories where homeowners could indulge their new interest in growing plants. Outdoors, colorful displays of annual flowers in cast iron urns and in island beds brightened both front and back gardens. This was the age of the gardenesque style, the Victorian adaptation of the earlier naturalistic approach to garden design.

The naturalistic garden style that swept England in the eighteenth century was firmly planted in the American consciousness by the mid-nineteenth century. This approach espoused lush and romantic effects—flowing curved lines, unclipped shrubs and trees planted in large groups, and natural water features such as waterfalls or lakes, preferably serpentine-shaped. Topiary, geometric patterns, fountains, and rigid enclosures were banished as too formal and unnatural. The gardenesque style was a refinement or offshoot of the naturalistic, with the same romantic lushness combined with exotic specimen trees, bright annuals planted in ornate patterns in island beds, cast iron urns and sculpture, and rustic furniture. It was an eclectic style that combined natural features and bright colors with a mood of mystery and romance.

Andrew Jackson Downing, a young and successful nurseryman working in Newburgh, New York, popularized the gardenesque style in the United States. Downing's great landscape book, *Treatise on the Theory and Practice of Landscape Gardening,* was published in 1841 and re-printed numerous times, the last edition being issued in 1921. It has had an incalculable effect on the design of the American landscape. In reaction to

A Spanish-style courtyard, above, provides sun, shade, and privacy for year-round outdoor living. The grand scale of Victorian houses, right, called for foundation planting to tie the house to the ground. Cast-iron planters, left, filled with bright flowers, were a favorite decoration in Victorian front gardens.

growing urbanism and industrialization, Downing wanted the landscape to give the illusion of nature unsullied. Influenced by the English garden writers and designers Humphry Repton and J. C. Loudon, Downing advocated undulating lawns, curving paths, groups of dark-foliaged evergreens to create "thickets, glades, and underwood, as in nature," and water features such as ponds, streams, and waterfalls. Specimen trees with interesting foliage, such as purple beech, were desirable.

The influence of Downing's naturalistic ideal is still seen in American suburbs today, and his approach is still the admired and approved style for many suburban properties. Houses are set back from the street; in the front, sweeps of adjoining lawns, interspersed with clumps of shrubs and trees, wipe out most evidence of property lines. Paths and driveways curve and swoop. The overall effect is of many houses arranged in a large park. However, the result of this influence is that the stamp of individuality is missing from the front of individual properties. So are privacy and gardens.

Two developments in the mid-nineteenth century that contributed to the look of the gardenesque property were the invention of the lawnmower, which made it possible to have vast areas of carefully tended grass, and the introduction of foundation planting, which was necessary to soften the tall foundations of Victorian houses.

THE LAWN

D O W N I N G, writing in 1854, extolled the virtue of lawn: "Grass . . . softened and refined by the frequent touches of the patient mower, until at last it becomes a perfect wonder of tufted freshness and verdure. . . . The great elements, then, of landscape gardening, as we understand it, are trees and grass." Frank J. Scott, one of the first landscape architects in America, in *The Art of Beautifying Suburban Home Grounds* (1870), wrote, "A smooth, closely shaven surface of grass is by far the most essential element of beauty on the grounds of the suburban house." And so the American love of beautiful lawns was born. Alice Morse Earle mourned the development of lawns, for they replaced the old front yard gardens she loved. In *Old Time Gardens* she wrote, "When the fences disappeared with the night rambles of the cows, the front yards gradually changed character; the tender blooms vanished, but the tall shrubs and the Peonies and Flower de Luce sturdily grew and blossomed, save where that dreary destroyer of a garden crept in— the desire for a lawn. The result was then a meagre expanse of poorly kept grass, with no variety, color or change —neither lawn nor front yard."

FOUNDATION PLANTING

F O U N D A T I O N planting, introduced in the mid-nineteenth century, seems to be a peculiarly American phenomenon. Before that time, as in Europe, American houses stood on their own. The rounded tops of large trees framed the house and softened the line of the roof against the sky. The foundation of the house was generally low, though houses in the South were sometimes raised for ventilation. The house was its own artistic entity, designed to be pleasing in proportion to its landscape and to people.

The immense scale and fussiness of Victorian houses, however, cried out for sizable plantings to tie them down,

and homeowners responded with shrubbery. Typically, large evergreen shrubs were planted on either side of the porch and at the front corners of the house. The spaces between were usually filled in with a line of shrubs. Depending on the climate, yew or holly might be used, which, as they grew, often were clipped into large gumdrop shapes. Rhododendrons and camellias were also popular, as were shrubs with variegated foliage. A yellow-variegated euonymus, aucuba, or privet brightened many foundations, and smaller evergreen shrubs filled out the space. Often a cast iron urn was planted with bright flowers, preferably red, a favorite color at this time. Island beds set in the lawn with elaborate designs of bright, bedded-out flowers completed the picture.

After the turn of the century, when great tracts of land were developed, foundation planting came into its own. In 1927, Frank A. Waugh's book, *Foundation Planting,* suggested its purposes: "First of all, the foundation planting should connect the house with the grounds and with other plantings. . . . after the foundation plantings have become established, the house then seems

Overgrown foundation planting, above left, can overwhelm and obscure a house. California poppies and sweet William have "jumped the fence," below left, making a brilliant tapestry between the street and sidewalk. The American passion for lawns, above, makes a parklike setting for houses.

to have grown out of the ground. Secondly, the foundation plantings should soften harsh architectural lines of the house." He concludes, "Finally, the foundation plantings help to dress up the whole place. . . . It makes it seem more cozy and homelike." These words were taken to heart by American gardeners and developers, and foundation plantings became ubiquitous in front yards. Developers and builders use foundation planting to give tract houses some feeling of permanence, and subsequent owners apparently can't bear to remove a shrub, or don't have another idea, so the shrubs are left in place to grow year after year. Many such foundation plantings have now outlived their usefulness and are blocking the windows and obliterating the lines of the houses.

· Reactions Against the Open Lawn ·

ALTHOUGH open lawns and foundation plantings became dominant features of suburban front yards, they were not universally admired. In his book *The American Gardener*, Allen

Lacy quotes several indignant authors. Grace Tabor wrote in 1921, "So a kind of landscape gardening has been attempted, in a loose fashion, to which boundary fences and walls . . . have been sacrificed in the vain hope of creating an illusion of the spaciousness and splendor which the town or suburban place cannot . . . possibly enjoy." And Neltje Blanchan in 1909 complained that "in an emotional moment of 'civic improvement' we were advised to take down our front fences and hedges, throw open our lawns and share with the public all the beauty of our home grounds, or be branded as selfish and undemocratic." She also complained about the disappearance of "the hedge . . . without which the perfect freedom of home life is no more possible than if the family living-room were to be set on a public stage." These various protests seem to have fallen on deaf ears.

· Toward a Synthesis ·

IN the economic boom of the late 1950s, tract housing, automobiles, roads, and sidewalks proliferated. This is when California landscape designers and thinkers, led by Garrett Eckbo and Thomas Church, got into full swing. The California school, as they came to be called, were modernists who addressed the question of good design at reasonable cost. Where outdoor living was possible most of the year, it was crucial to separate private recreation space from parking, entrances, and streets. Screening, decks, and terraces were freely used in the home landscapes designed by the Californians. The front garden was often small, just a separation between sidewalk and house. Recognizing that grass was not the most practical groundcover in a climate with dry summers, the designers experimented with native plants adapted to local conditions. The often rugged terrain led to innovative designs, with gardens, drives, and parking sometimes placed on different levels, and with decks and pools cantilevered over hillsides.

In most of the United States, though, the situation remained as it had been through the sixties. Open, democratic front yards, neighborhoods with continuous, parklike planting, and very little personality displayed in gardens in the front of the house were the norm. But in the 1970s several factors came into play that changed homeowners' ideas of how their property would be used. More people have taken up gardening, and today the front yard is sometimes the best, or even the only, place for a garden or pool. Land prices have shot up, and houses are being built on ever smaller parcels of land, where each inch must be put to use. And the rise of postmodern architecture in the 1970s and '80s, with its design motifs from the past, has brought renewed interest in fences, entrance courts, and porte-cochères on the front property.

We have entered a period of synthesis in American landscaping. Homeowners and gardeners are becoming aware of the necessity and availability of good design as it relates to their own property. Pools, terraces, walks, and driveways, as well as gardens, are being integrated into overall landscape design schemes. And the front yard is being looked at as an opportunity for creativity, rather than the obligatory anonymous, parklike setting of the past.

EVALUATING THE FRONT PROPERTY

Stone steps curving through a hillside garden make a commanding entrance. Large hemlocks at the crest of the hill add a further dimension of height. Steep sites are easy to maintain when planted with groundcover and bulbs rather than lawn.

*F*OR any number of reasons, the front of your house and property, whether brand new or a hundred years old, may need to be perked up, redesigned, and reorganized. Perhaps new plantings will make the house look more attractive, or you may want to put the unused space in the front to a better purpose. If you need a place to grow flowers or vegetables and the front of the house is the sunniest area, you might consider planting a cottage garden at the front door. If you are tired of looking at a large garage door and several cars every time you go in or out of the house, perhaps shrubs and flowers can distract the eye from the garage and parking areas. Or maybe you'd like to have more privacy from the street, or a quiet place to relax or read outside on a pleasant day.

· Taking Stock ·

T H E essential first step in rethinking your front yard is to analyze what you have and what you want to do. Make a list of the elements already present on your property, such as a garage, a driveway, or an herb garden. Then make a list of what you would like to add, such as a storage shed or a swimming pool. Some items on your list may reflect your desire to improve the appearance of the front yard. For instance, "Sprucing up the parking area" might be a consideration. This wish list may have more items on it than your front property or budget will actually accommodate. When the list is complete, you should rank the items in order of importance. If you have children, remember that they will use a pool or tennis court a great deal, and so will their friends. So it is best to make

such additions while the children are still at home to enjoy them.

Any major project, such as a pool, new drive, or terrace, which requires heavy machinery that will tear up some of your yard, should be done first. There is no sense putting in a new garden by the garage and later adding a new drive that necessitates tearing up everything in the vicinity. Be open-minded when considering where major additions can be placed; pools and terraces need not necessarily be at the back of the house. If the front is the sunniest part of your property, think about putting the pool or terrace there. Don't be intimidated; you can always add hedges or fencing for privacy.

Perimeter or privacy plantings should be done at an early stage. Most shrubs take at least five to ten years to reach an effective size, so they should be given a head start. Once these major improvements have been made, smaller gardens and specimen plants can be put in as time and money allow.

PRACTICALITIES

A primary consideration in analyzing

your front garden is function. The front yard usually contains most of the property's utility and service areas. A garage or carport, an area for parking, a driveway, an area for garbage storage and pickup, and paths to the front and kitchen doors are generally located in the front or side yard. Do these structures function as well as you would like them to? Could you move the box that holds the garbage cans out of sight and still get at them easily? Could you rearrange the space so you won't have to move other cars to get your car out? Could you hide or disguise part of the parking area? Could the space absorb, and would local ordinances permit, construction of a small storage building for garbage cans as well as for the various bicycles, sleds, and gardening tools that are now cluttering the garage or, worse yet, the carport, where your junk is in full view? Remember the importance of good lighting, which allows you to move safely from the car to the house at night. Part of the job of designing the front yard is to make sure all the necessary practical functions are adequately provided for in an attractive way.

THE EAGLE EYE

A F T E R you consider all the functional needs, take an objective look at your property. This may be hard to do because you are so used to seeing your house and grounds; you go in and out without really looking. One way to get a fresh perspective is to find new vantage points. Walk across the street and surprise yourself by turning around to look at your place as though you are seeing it for the first time. Think how it must look to a visitor who's never been there before. Go to your neighbor's yard and porch and take another look. Also study neighboring properties. How do the layout and plantings compare and relate to yours? What do you like or dislike, what is different, what is the same?

As part of your analysis, consider how your front garden and house relate to others on your street. Is your house one of many designed and built at the same time and set in an uninterrupted flow of lawn along the whole block? If all the front areas are essentially a single landscape, careful planning will be necessary to assure that your scheme

Garden styles can be as varied as the houses they front. A planted roof is part of the dramatic landscape at a seaside house, *top*, where wind- and salt-tolerant plants contribute to the rugged sense of place. In July and August masses of hydrangeas hold their own against the large stone and shingle entrance of a summer house, *above*. Boxwood, roses on a picket fence, topiary, and flowers planted in patterns are themes for a traditional entrance garden, *right*.

isn't obtrusive. If you don't want your property to stick out like a sore thumb, one way to provide a visual reference is to repeat in your garden plants already used in the neighborhood. Using materials, colors, and styles that relate to the other houses will also help integrate your landscape into the rest of the neighborhood. If, on the other hand, you live on a street with a hodgepodge of house styles and essentially separate landscaping, you will have more freedom of choice.

THE SURVEY

Y O U or your lawyer should have a copy of the survey that was made when you bought your property. This will show you the lot size, the position and dimensions of the house, and the exact boundaries of the property. The local planning office will explain the setbacks and building limitations for your area. Most communities now have setback regulations specifying the distances allowed between structures and the property lines. Additional regulations may govern the height of the fences and hedges at the front of the property and their distance from the property line.

Have the survey enlarged at a copy store and make several copies so you can experiment with ideas for rearranging your property. Garden writer Linda Yang has a suggestion for sketching outdoors: tape a copy of the survey to a firm surface such as cardboard so it doesn't blow around as you take measurements and make notes. Use one color ink for existing structures that will remain and a second color for your proposed additions. The survey is a useful tool for determining exactly how much space you have to play with.

· *Finding the Right Style* ·

M A N Y factors influence the appearance of your home ground. The style and scale of the house, natural features of the site, and geographic characteristics all have some bearing on the style of your garden. In the introduction to her book *Gardens for Small Country Houses*, written in 1912, Gertrude Jekyll states, "It is grievous to see, in a place that has some well-defined natural character, that character destroyed or stultified, for it is just that quality that is the most precious." She goes on to explain the importance of using naturally occurring plants in a site with strong character rather than "common nursery stuff."

Jekyll advises letting the character of a garden be dictated by the topography and existing trees. On a hilly site, make the most of the drama of the rocks and the shape of the land. Use plants to enhance the natural features, not hide them. It is important that the whole property express the character of the landscape, whatever that may be.

Relating the style of the garden to the style of the house is also crucial to a successful, integrated landscape. A mountain chalet in the woods or a rustic cottage near a sand dune should have a naturalistic garden suitable to the locale. Shrubs, trees, and flowers that thrive in the local conditions should be planted rather casually, emulating the existing natural vegetation. Paths should be wood or rough stone, not more refined brick or bluestone, the materials of towns and suburbs. Conversely, if you have an elegant Tudor or Georgian house, the planting

and the landscaping materials that make up the paths and terraces should be dignified and the layout somewhat formal. A large shingle house might have tall trees, hedges, well-maintained lawns, and a formal terrace.

A very simple farm house or a contemporary house with plain lines calls for landscaping in a similar mood. For a modern one-story house you might choose a Japanese-inspired garden with understated plantings and a clear, rectangular structure. A discreet gate in a fence that conceals the front yard from the street hints that a garden is inside. Such a garden is subdued and depends on a few specimen plants for drama.

Availability of sun will also affect the style of the garden. A site with many large trees will generally have a woodsy, informal garden with loose groups of shade-loving shrubs, ferns, hostas, wildflowers, and groundcovers. Formal gardens appropriate to a shady site can be designed using shade-tolerant evergreen shrubs such as yew, holly, or boxwood, clipped to emphasize the lines of planting beds. Careful design can successfully combine the loose shapes of woodsy plants and

The spirit of an entrance garden should suit the site and the architectural style of the house. In the desert a path curves through the dramatic forms of an indigenous cactus garden, top. At a contemporary house, above, glass walls provide a view of the garden, which doubles as the entrance to the house. Brilliant phlox on the front fence of a house on a ranch, above right, compete with the sky and mountains for attention. An Oriental mood is evoked by clipped pines, stone lanterns, gravel, and boulders, below right.

shrubs with strong character to make the garden appropriate to the style of the house.

The site will also influence the style of your front yard. Land that is relatively flat and unencumbered by such natural elements as boulders allows greater freedom of choice in the garden layout than a steep, craggy hill. If you do have significant natural features, it is best to let them determine the style of the garden.

FORMAL OR INFORMAL?

F O R any house, suburban, city, or country, the primary style question is formal or informal, open or closed? The debate over the effectiveness of formal versus informal style is a continuing one in American landscape design. Traditionally the front garden has been more formal than the area in back of the house, where the occupants spend more time. In the back we feel protected from people passing by because we have the mass of the house to give us privacy. The back is where we sit, have a barbecue, play sports, and perhaps have a swimming pool. It is a place for casual outdoor living. Shrubs

and flower beds may be planted around the perimeter, and perhaps a vegetable plot is tucked behind a fence. Because the back yard is private, its style is apt to be more personal. We can create what we like without comment from the rest of the world.

Front gardens, in contrast, tend to follow a formula developed at the turn of the century and not reconsidered for years. The "proper" front-of-the-house planting style includes some evergreens lined up along the foundation, a walk, a light, and perhaps some groundcover. It is anonymous and impersonal, rather formal, as though the area were used only for ritual entering and leaving. So what is an appropriate garden style for the front, public side of your house and property? The options may be more varied than you think. A wild garden or meadow right at the front door might not be appropriate, unless you live in a farmhouse on acres of open land. But you could grow wildflowers in a structured setting, combining carefully designed and constructed paths and beds with loose masses of shrubs, flowers, and ornamental grasses.

The front of any house has paths, a drive, and boundaries, which by their nature are structured and formal. These formal elements are necessary to the proper organization of the home ground. Beatrix Farrand, the great American garden designer and writer, gives us useful guidance on the formal approach when describing her design, done in 1910, for a competition called "An Ideal Suburban Place."

No attempt has been made at an informal or so called naturalistic treatment because on a lot less than half an acre in size . . . irregular lines, winding walks and scattered trees would only look crowded without giving any illusion of space. Honesty and clearness of design are perhaps even more necessary in the treatment of the small places than they are in larger areas, where the size of the grounds alone gives a suggestion of distancy which is impossible to ever obtain in a little lot. Here a frank recognition of the boundary line is essential.

The plantings on most American suburban properties have been designed with a philosophy that is the opposite of Beatrix Farrand's. Informal, irregular plantings blur the boundary lines, suggesting that the property extends into the distance. Whether this approach is effective when a neighboring house can actually be seen nearby is open to debate.

BOUNDARIES

T H E front of a property has numerous boundary lines. There is the line of the sidewalk, which marks where a private piece of land ends and public space begins. And beyond the sidewalk, where pedestrians, bikers, and skaters hold sway, is the curb, marking where cars belong. On the two sides of the plot the property lines may be carefully delineated by fencing or clipped hedges, although in suburban locations they are apt to be less distinct. Clumps of shrubs and trees straddling the boundary line indicate approximately where your land abuts the neighbors'. You can create additional boundaries in the front of your property. Sectioning off areas with fences or hedges and gates is essential if major additions are to be made. For example, if you are putting in a swimming pool, a fence will provide privacy and safety. Analyzing how

the various components of your front yard work or don't work is the first step in figuring out what changes will improve your front yard. The next step is working out a realistic plan.

· Making Your Ideas Work ·

A F T E R you've decided what you'd like to accomplish, you'll want to know whether your new design will look pleasing. As you drive or walk around your town, find one or two house fronts you like. Stop and note what is appealing—layout, paths, structures, plants—not to copy someone else's design slavishly but to provide a jumping-off point for your own ideas. Maybe you will see an attractive path or style of steps, or perhaps the way part of the front yard is sectioned off would be just the thing at your place.

Photos are another source of ideas. Garden design books and garden magazines have proliferated in the last five years and can give you many solutions or partial solutions to consider. By

A cottage with a dramatic view of sky and water calls for simple treatment at the entrance. Rocks, junipers, and yews are brightened by annuals.

studying a picture in a book or magazine, or a photograph you have taken, you can get a good feeling of what materials, proportions, and layout make the landscape or structure attractive. If you buy magazines, make a file of pictures you tear out so you can refer to them easily. When you find a picture you like in a book, mark it with a Post-It™ note so you can find it quickly later.

In *The Principles of Gardening,* Hugh Johnson suggests drawing proposed changes on a photograph with a black felt-tip marker. Take several photos of the front of your property, preferably in black and white, as color can be distracting. Have the photos enlarged to at least 8 by 10 inches. Draw in the hedges, walks, and trees you want to add in various combinations and configurations. Play with the arrangement of elements. Try a couple of designs that seem a little kooky—you might find some unexpected solutions to your landscape problems. You can also experiment with eliminating elements from the photos. Use white correction fluid (sold in stationery stores) to cover a tree or shrub that you're thinking of removing, then draw in what you might plant to replace it.

Another way to draw ideas is to tape acetate sheets over the photograph. Use felt tip markers or crayons to put in and take out trees, groupings of shrubs, or paths. This will give you a more realistic sense than a one-dimensional ground plan will of what the landscaping will look like.

DO YOU NEED A DESIGNER?

Y O U may want a garden designer or landscape architect to plan and plant your new landscape, or you may prefer to do it yourself with some general suggestions on how to proceed. If you plan to add a large, permanent structure, such as a patio or pool, a professional's input on siting can be all-important. Too often a homeowner has a pool installed in whatever location the contractor suggests, and then can't figure out why it doesn't look as though it belongs. Proper siting—considering how the new structure will relate to the rest of the landscaping and where it will look best and function properly— is essential.

There are some general guidelines to follow in deciding whether you need the services of a landscape architect or a garden designer. Landscape architects are trained in construction and design. They generally have less familiarity with plants than garden designers. When a project involves earth moving, grading, construction, and large-scale redesign, as for a swimming pool or new driveway, a landscape architect is probably called for.

You may want to hire a garden designer if you are adding a perennial border or thoroughly reorganizing your property. Garden designers are generally very knowledgeable about plants; they may also have some design background, but it will not be as technical as a landscape architect's. Usually, a landscape architect does construction in the landscape, while a garden designer is concerned with organization of the landscape and the arrangement of plants.

For a fee, most designers will come for a consultation and write up their suggestions for you to use as a guide. How do you find a designer you'll enjoy working with? Most nurseries and garden centers have designers on the staff. Some designers advertise in the classified section of local newspapers, or friends may know a designer or have

used one themselves. Talk to several designers or landscape architects and ask to see their portfolios. When you have discussed their ideas and looked at their photos, you can ask one or two whose work you like to show you a job they have done for another client. A designer and client who have had a successful relationship are generally happy to discuss a job, its problems and limitations. If you have seen garden designs that you feel are appropriate for you and your site, all this research won't be necessary. Choose someone whose work you like.

If you don't feel you need the services of a design professional, it can be useful to try out your ideas on friends, neighbors, and family. They will see things differently from you and may suggest details and problems you haven't considered. You don't have to take anyone else's advice; ultimately the decisions are yours. Consider it information gathering and use only the ideas you like. It is better to think about the project from as many angles as possible before you begin than to find yourself in the unhappy position of saying, "Wish I'd thought of that!" when the work is done. Knowing what

Walls delineate boundaries. Brick walls make an intimate dooryard, above. The direct line of the path through the wall to the door is a clear invitation to enter. A rough stone wall, above left, separates field from flower garden. A wall and gate of wood and bamboo, below left, encloses a Japanese garden.

you don't want ("I don't want cars at the front door" or "I don't want a walk bisecting the front yard") will help you define and achieve what you do want.

TRY IT OUT

C H A N G E S to the structure of a garden seem so permanent and definite. Moving plants and structures outdoors is not like moving furniture; you don't have the option of putting the plants and structures back if you don't like the new arrangement. So if you are still not sure your ideas make sense or if they will look good, build some models. Use stakes and string to lay out paths or terraces. Make sure the path is wide enough for two people to walk on, that there is plenty of room for greetings and farewells at the door, that a terrace will accommodate a table and bench or chairs or whatever else you want to have on it.

Bob Dash, a noted Long Island artist and gardener, suggests throwing a sheet or drop cloth over a chair to get the effect of a shrub. Move the covered chair around the yard to help you visualize a new shrub in various locations. Tall stakes hammered into the ground with string running between can give an approximation of a hedge or fence. I have used a chaise longue on its side with a beach towel thrown over it to see if a hedge looks right in the position I was considering. If you try out all these things in front of the house, the neighbors will probably stream out to see if you are moving out or are about to ruin the block. Bring them into your project—remember, two heads are better than one.

DRAWINGS

I F you hire a professional designer to work on your property, he or she will give you a schematic plan of the job with all buildings, paths, drives, and proposed plantings (see the case studies in Chapter 5 for some examples of plans). Drawings are an important tool for organizing property and plants. They give you a good sense of how one part of the yard will relate to another. Paths going to the house can be seen clearly, and the importance of a planting bed that connects a porch to a gate becomes apparent on paper. Be warned, though, that it can be difficult to visualize how a one-dimensional plan with a bird's eye perspective will look in elevation. If you ask, the designer will probably be glad to draw an elevation showing how the various vertical elements relate to each other. Or the designer may help you lay out sticks and string to see where the paths and beds will go.

· Thinking About the Budget ·

Y O U R budget is an important consideration, too. If you can't afford all the changes you would like to make, rank your projects in order of priority and spread them out over several years. Before you do anything else, you'll want to find out what your landscaping projects will cost. If you plan to act as your own contractor, get the names of reputable pool, fencing, and garden contractors from friends and neighbors who have been pleased with their work. Get at least two estimates for any project. You must provide specific information in order to get a realistic bid. For a pool, you need to know the approximate size you want, the kind of decking for the surround, and whether there will be any extras, such as a diving board. You may have to modify your ideal design somewhat once the prices come in.

If you hire a garden designer or landscape architect, that person's job is to help you come up with a complete plan for the work to be done and to get bids for work. It also includes supervising construction and installation to make sure the work is done according to specifications. Hiring a designer is more expensive than doing the job yourself, of course, because you are paying for the designer's time. The advantage is that the designer, because of his or her contacts, should be able to get the job done quickly and properly. If you don't have time to oversee the work, it can be an advantage to have someone supervising for you.

When you evaluate the front property, think about how it is now used or not used, and how a new design will change that. Once you identify the changes that will make your place operate more smoothly, consider how to make the new arrangements visually pleasing. Enhanced by new hedges, fences, walks, and gardens, the front property will look better and perform better.

APPROACHES AND TRANSITIONS

Paths are an invitation to the mind and feet to follow along, to see what is ahead. The line of the path, as well as its pattern, is important. Here blocks of bricks laid in sand carry visitors through a garden and around the corner to a new vista.

RRIVALS are important. When a visitor crosses the line from public to private space, there should be a feeling of anticipation. What lies ahead? What flowers will be in bloom? Who is at home? It is important to put your own stamp on the design of the entrance area, to make it personal. As garden designer Grace Tabor wrote in 1911: "The entrance gives to the whole place its characteristic first impression."

Too often the vista one encounters when entering a property is a gaping garage door. If the object of your landscaping is to make the approach to the house more attractive, stop in the middle of the driveway and take a good look at what you see. Pretend you are a prospective house buyer. Would this first impression please you? If not, what would you like to see instead?

The most heavily and frequently used parts of the front of the property are the driveway and parking area and the family entrance to the house. Family members leave and enter the driveway in cars several times a day. The garbage collector, delivery people, and visitors may stop in at any time of day. So this service area must be carefully thought out to function well and must be carefully designed to look as good as it can, given that its components aren't usually inherently attractive.

Although driveways and paths may seem more related to architecture than to horticulture, planning their locations provides the framework around which the front garden will be designed. It is a necessary prelude to designing the actual garden. The driveway and adjoining paths carry us from the large public spaces of streets and sidewalks to the intimacy of the entrance and the home, providing a psychological and visual transition from outside to inside. When they are well made and attractively planted, we feel welcome.

· Consider the Driveway ·

BECAUSE they are so frequently used and so important, the parking area and entrances of the front or side of the house should function smoothly and adequately, preferably in an attractive way. Why be confronted every day with asphalt, open garage doors, and a dreary back stoop, unrelieved by the softening of planting?

Cars are to the landscape what television sets are to interior decor—an unattractive necessity. For better or for worse, our lives are structured around these machines. People have come up with various ways of dealing with televisions and cars. TVs can be stored in an armoire or cabinet with closed doors, just as a car is stored in a garage. But the garage is often the outdoor equipment storage area as well, and older children may have cars of their own, so some cars are often visible when family members are at home. We don't need to pretend that cars don't exist; let's just not let them dominate our outdoor decor.

PLANTING THE ENTRANCE

T H E point at which the driveway leaves the street and enters your property makes a statement about the thought that has gone into the design of the drive and, indeed, the whole property. This is the area first encountered by people coming to your house by car. Is it welcoming? A post with the house number or name is helpful. A pair of attractive pillars invites visitors to enter. A group of shrubs often marks the entrance drive, although too often this arrangement, like foundation planting, has become a cliché with a few tired, overgrown junipers or yews.

The planting at the entrance to the drive can give a hint of the style of the rest of the house and garden. Most people leave the drive entrance simple and unobtrusive because that is the style of their front landscaping. However, if you are looking for a place to display horticultural talents, this is one. The design can be as flamboyant or sub-dued as you like—just remember that you are creating a first impression. A pair of conifers flanking the drive entrance makes an elegant statement and clearly indicates the way in. In the Southwest cactuses can make a direct, dramatic statement. A mixed grouping of evergreen shrubs, small flowering shrubs, and perennials and annuals for color creates a garden for all passersby to enjoy. You might consider junipers for all-season interest and small flowering shrubs like daphne, spirea, or even some polyantha or rugosa roses, underplanted with spring bulbs, to form the backbone of an entrance garden. With the addition of decorative grasses of striking color and dramatic inflorescence, such as *Helictotrichon sempervirens*, and some colorful annuals, you have a garden with year-round interest. I have specifically not suggested azaleas and rhododendrons as driveway plantings because they have been overused in exactly such situations. Diversity is needed!

SURFACE AND LAYOUT

T H E next impression to consider is that made by the layout and surface of

Fences and gates create transitions between public and private space. A post and light make a welcoming entrance, above. A fence and gate design by Cooper, Robertson and Partners, above right, separates parking from garden. Steps beside the drive, below right, lead through a stucco wall.

the driveway. By designing the driveway to relate to the style of the house and landscaping, you will create a unified appearance. Repetition of one of the materials used in the house helps make the design coherent. With a brick house, for example, you might edge the driveway with brick or construct a brick-paved parking area. Likewise, stone edging or surfacing that repeats the stone used in the house or in the surrounding landscape makes a visual connection, both in style and material, to the rest of the picture. Such elegant solutions to the design of the driveway are likely to be found on an architect-designed site where the house and landscape have been built at the same time.

Most driveways have a cement, asphalt, or gravel surface. Fine gravel is more refined looking than large gravel, and the visual effect of each kind should be weighed when choosing a gravel surface. On a practical note, consider whether your drive must be plowed frequently in the winter. Gravel gets pushed around during plowing, and for that reason you may decide on another surface. Metal edging helps

keep a gravel drive neat, but it is important to install it so it is unobtrusive. The edging should act as a barrier to grass roots and not protrude above the surface of the drive more than an inch and a half.

If your existing driveway functions well but isn't made of the material you'd select if given a choice, try adding some strategically placed planting or fencing to block out your view of the drive from the house and the rest of the property. A visual barrier such as a fence, trellis, low hedge, or flower bed can soften the appearance of an ugly driveway.

On properties larger than half an acre, it used to be deemed practical to have a U-shaped drive passing by the front door with two entrances to the street, or to have a circle at the front door so you can drive around and rejoin the driveway. Such designs take up a lot of space—a car needs at least 60 or 70 feet to turn easily—and separate the entire front of the property from the rest of the land. The front yard essentially becomes the driveway. If your landscaping goal is to have more space for gardens and recreation, a large drive

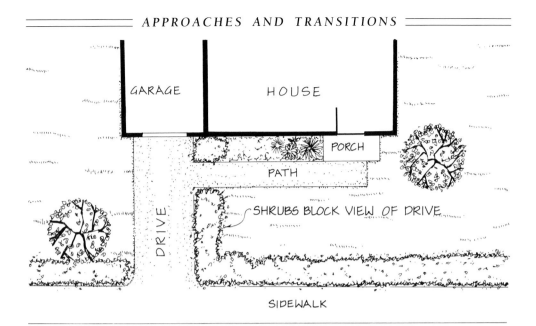

A driveway that dominates the view can be concealed with simple shrub plantings.

taking up a major part of the front yard should not be part of the scheme.

When laying out a driveway, simplicity is best. Getting from the street to the parking area should be done directly if possible. A straight drive to the parking area or garage, with ample area to turn and park, is generally satisfactory. If your property is large or hilly, however, the drive may curve—gently so that steering isn't an effort. Perhaps there is a natural feature or vista that can be appreciated if you route the drive indirectly. In this way you can create the pleasant impression of driving on a country lane.

· Parking, Garages, and Service Buildings ·

I F your property is small and the garage is close to the street, chances are you back out into the street, turn, and drive off. Extra cars and those of visitors are parked on the street. You cannot change that situation unless you own enough land next to the drive to make a turning area. If the street is little traveled, you may want to leave the driveway as is and consider planting or fencing between the drive and the front yard. But if traffic on your street makes backing and turning in the street diffi-

Imaginative gardeners can turn a garage into an opportunity for planting. Hanging baskets of geraniums and a tub of pansies, above, enhance the driveway and garage door. A garden of yuccas, berberis, and junipers, left, helps disguise an unused garage door. Twining clematis and honeysuckle and a cluster of pots on the steps, right, transform a dull door into a romantic entrance.

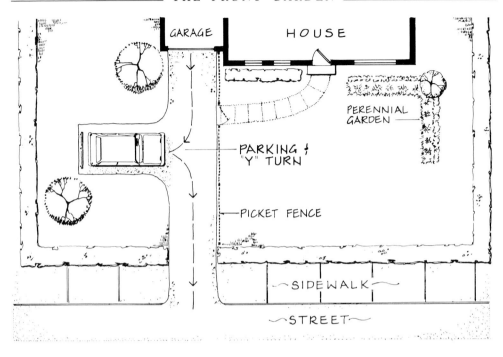

GARAGE HOUSE

PERENNIAL GARDEN

PARKING & "Y" TURN

PICKET FENCE

~SIDEWALK~

~STREET~

Creating a slot for parking and turning makes the driveway more useful.

cult, a turning Y is a good idea, assuming there is space. This arrangement takes up relatively little space and can double as a parking place for visitors. Made wider, the backing area can serve as a permanent parking place. You need an area about 15 by 20 feet next to the driveway to maneuver the car. A log or some stones at the end of the turning area will keep visitors from driving their cars onto the lawn.

A long driveway may provide more possibilities for masking the garage and parking areas. If the drive passes a side door to the house and continues to a garage, a porte-cochère over the drive will partially hide the garage beyond, provide a place to stop in the rain, and add visual emphasis to the side door.

PLANT OUT THE PARKING AREA

W H E N you need parking for several cars, try to arrange the area in such a way that it is partially masked by plantings. If possible, angle the space so that when you walk out of the house you aren't looking at the tail ends of three or four cars lined up like a used car lot. If the parking area is at right angles to the house, rather than parallel to it, a

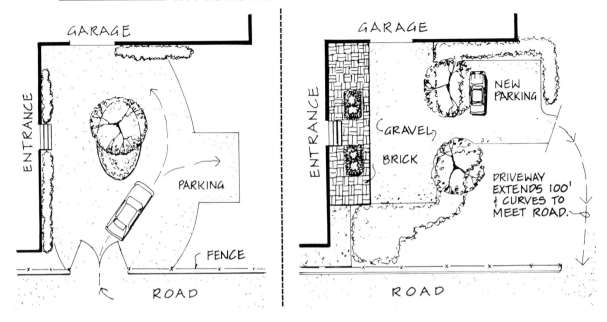

Redesigning a parking area to hide cars from view. Before, left, parking is opposite the front door. After, right, parking is concealed by shrubs. The driveway, the only access to the property, enters at a new angle.

few shrubs will block the cars and minimize their impact.

If you cannot change the orientation of the parking area, try to figure out a way to use plants to conceal the garage and parking area from the house entrance. Perhaps there is space for a garden on either side of the doorstep with a path leading from the house to the parking area. Even a clump of shrubs on the edge of the parking area will shield the view of the cars somewhat.

What if you live on a steep or difficult site and the only place to park is right in front of the entrance to the house? If there will always be a car or

two there and no amount of juggling will change the situation, the only solution is to make the area as attractive as possible. The surface of the parking area doesn't have to be macadam or gravel. A brick parking court with vertical conifers at the corners and evergreen shrubs edging the sides is always pleasant to look at. If cars are likely to bump into shrubs, using a groundcover such as myrtle or ivy for the edging will give you more leeway when turning the car. Think of using a variegated groundcover, such as a gold-centered ivy. Plants in the driveway area should be chosen for variety of leaf color, dis-

Service buildings near the entrance to a house can be disguised with plants. Grapevines range over a pergola on the front of a storage shed, above. A box topped by a tub of morning glories, near right, encloses an electric meter. A lean-to for garbage cans, far right, hides behind a stand of hollyhocks.

tinctive branch structure, and winter interest; it is just as important to have well-thought-out plantings here as on the rest of the property.

At a rustic house in the country or in a suburb that purposely retains a rural feeling, a parking court paved with large, textured stones is handsome. A round stone in the center of the court with irregular stones radiating out from it makes a visually interesting surface for an arrival and parking area.

It is also possible to make a lawn parking area using honeycomb pavers designed for grass to grow through. The interlocking honeycombs, made of high-density plastic, are strong enough

to be driven on; their structure gives a car traction even when the grass is wet. The grass can be mowed like a conventional lawn. The pavers provide a tough surface for extra parking spots near or adjoining the driveway. These kinds of design solutions, interesting to look at as well as functional, rise above the humdrum.

BAN CARS

O N E somewhat radical solution to the parking problem, probably best adopted only by those desperate for garden space, is to ban cars from the property completely and turn over to

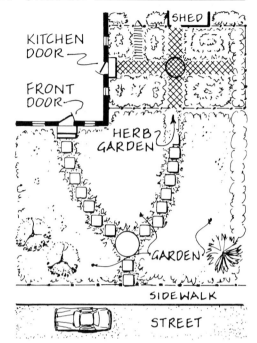

On a small property a garden replaces a garage and drive. Parking is on the street.

horticulture the space formerly used for driveway, parking, and garage. This solution works for weekend and summer homes, for the young and energetic, or for those living in warm, dry climates. With the car parked on the street, paths to the front door and perhaps the kitchen door can pass through a beautiful garden where the driveway once was. This arrangement generally works best on a small plot with the house close to the street.

WHAT ABOUT THE GARAGE DOOR?

T H E R E is no denying the practicality of being able to drive straight into the garage or parking area and step easily into the house with loads of groceries, particularly in cold and wet weather. However, if you are tired of looking into the garage as you drive up your driveway, consider whether the garage entrance could be closed off and a new entrance created around the corner. The attraction of this idea is that the garage entrance and parking area can be shielded from view with strategically placed shrubs. Instead of the garage door, opened or closed, being the culmination of the view up the drive, the new view will be the wall of the garage, perhaps with a window, a trellis with roses, and a garden. Moving the garage entrance is definitely a big-ticket project and probably should be considered only if you are remodeling the house or garage.

SERVICE BUILDINGS DON'T HAVE TO BE UGLY

T H E driveway and parking area usually function as the service space, where equipment that doesn't belong in the house is organized and stored. There may be several structures to ac-

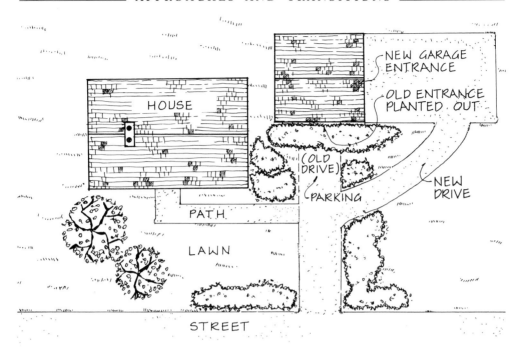

When a garage door dominates the view, it may be possible to reorient parking. If the garage can be entered from the side, a garden will conceal the old door.

commodate cars, tools, sports equipment, and garbage cans. A house in the country may have tanks for gas somewhere near the back. A beach house often has an outdoor shower and a line on which to hang bathing suits and beach towels. If these structures are built solidly, in a style that is compatible with and complementary to the house, they can be an asset instead of an ugly distraction.

With a colonial-style house, for instance, a painted shed or garage with one or two windows, perhaps with windowboxes and shutters all painted or stained to match the house, can be an aesthetic and practical addition to the property. It can act as a backdrop for a small garden bed, or you can train roses to ramble over it in the style of a Nantucket cottage. Garbage containers can be stored in the shed, or a wooden cupboard can be built on the side to accommodate them. Storing bikes in a bike rack against one wall of the shed is more pleasing than leaving the bikes on the ground. Enclosing an outdoor shower and drying yard with a fence or lattice attached to the side of the garage or shed is a discreet solution.

The texture and material of a path should enhance the house entrance. A simple brick path and step, right, complement a shingle house. Wooden paths, top, were once common in lumber-rich western towns. Large blocks of stone, above, set in grass make a bold path.

· Create Transitions ·

G O O D architecture in the garden divides space appropriately, just as it does in a house. A hedge, fence, or garden at the driveway boundary visually and psychologically separates the parking area from the rest of the property. An opening in the fence or hedge is a passage from a public, functional space through an enclosure to another kind of outdoor space, a garden. Think of the transition as similar to that of walking from the kitchen, a work area with noisy, practical machines, to the living room, a place for sitting and talking or reading. Walls and a door make the kitchen and living room function separately, and the same is true in the landscape. When you walk through a gate or opening from the parking space to the house entrance area, you have the welcoming and protected feeling of arriving home.

THE NEED FOR PATHS

P A T H S create connections in the landscape. They gather the various parts of a garden together and link the house to the garden. Visually and practically, paths show us where to go. The hard surfaces create a foil for the lush, soft shapes of plants. Paths look and feel right when they are the same masonry materials used in the house or of native stone or wood. Where you put them and what they are made of are both important considerations.

First and foremost, paths must lead to the doors of the house. If you have isolated the parking area with a hedge or fence, a path must lead you through a gate or enclosure to a door. The path indicates where the entrance is and enables you to get there with dry feet in wet weather. The path to the door most frequently used in your household should be wide and authoritative. Stepping stones or a less important path can lead to a secondary door. Paths near the house should be direct and should be constructed of hard materials slightly pitched for good drainage.

If you have a large front lawn with a path down the middle, rethink this arrangement. Just as a circular drive sweeping in front of the porch robs space from the expanse of the front yard, so does a bisecting path. A better arrangement is to move the path to the

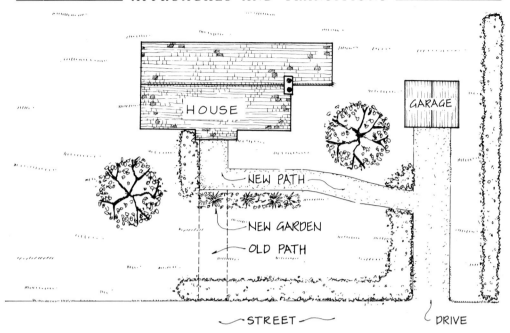

A front yard will feel more spacious and private when a bisecting path is moved. New plants create an enclosure at the front door.

side of the property, perhaps next to the driveway, and then make it curve or angle parallel to the front of the house, ending at the front door. You will have reclaimed the front yard for a garden or a place for your children to play football.

THE SURFACE IS IMPORTANT

P A T H S are expensive to build, and the materials you choose will affect the price. Stone and brick are durable and attractive but expensive to install. For a colonial house, brick is always suitable and offers endless possibilities for creating patterns. Brick can be laid in herringbone or basketweave patterns, or it can outline shapes such as diamonds or circles along the length of the path. Brick is suitable to both elegant and informal landscaping. Bluestone and fieldstone also make sturdy, handsome paths. Bluestone, often found in city gardens, is a sophisticated material. The rough texture of fieldstone makes it suitable for rustic schemes.

Concrete is a practical and less expensive option. You can make it more attractive by treating the surface to create texture. Brushing wet concrete or adding pebbles to the surface creates a

*Exuberant planting adds charm at an entrance.
A profusion of pots at a converted carriage
house, top, can be rearranged for seasonal
displays. Dense honeysuckle emphasizes the
architecture of the door, left. The entrance to
Ryan Gainey's garden, above right, through a
shady bower gives a glimpse of what is to come.
Rosalind Creasy's edible garden, below right,
spills onto the driveway and entrance path.*

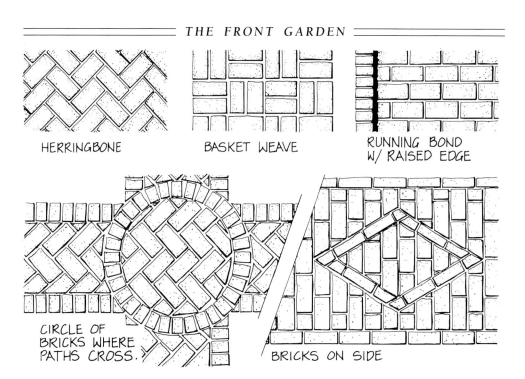

HERRINGBONE   BASKET WEAVE   RUNNING BOND
W/ RAISED EDGE

CIRCLE OF
BRICKS WHERE
PATHS CROSS.   BRICKS ON SIDE

Take advantage of the almost limitless configurations in which bricks can be laid to add year-round interest to paths and entrances.

pleasing visual effect. Joints of wood, brick, or stone set up a pleasing repetition and reduce the institutional feeling of this material. If you have a young child, don't forget to make an imprint of a hand or foot in a discreet place. The path will always hold a reminder of how small your children once were.

SECONDARY PATHS

SECONDARY paths perform other functions. At the front of the property, a narrow path leading off the major path from the drive to the entry, may carry you farther from the house.

A curving path will entice you to walk through a garden or orchard or to find out what is around a corner. A straight path, say between two perennial borders, may lead to an architectural feature or bench at the culmination of a vista. Secondary paths are for strolling and looking and can be made of softer materials suitable to the locale, such as bark chips, sawdust, gravel, or mowed grass.

· Kitchen Door versus Front Door ·

WHETHER the front door or the kitchen door is the focus of family life at your house, some special touches will make the entrance inviting. A porch with a roof, and perhaps some trellising with roses, morning glory, or clematis clambering up is welcoming. A cottage or country house sometimes has a bench built into the side of the porch, an invitation to sit down, take off your boots, and come in. Pots with seasonal flowers are a simple way to make the entrance attractive. Primroses, verbena, and geraniums can be rotated so that when one plant finishes blooming new ones are added to keep up the show. Ferns and begonias in pots make lush displays at a shaded entrance. Larger, more permanent tubs or pots planted with shrubs offer a more unusual arrangement. A shiny black planter with a dwarf blue spruce on its own or underplanted with seasonal flowers looks exciting. Furnishing an entrance with pots, tubs, and benches adds another dimension to the existing planting, paths, and steps.

WINTER INTEREST

B E sure to think about what the entrance will look like in winter. Evergreen plantings at the door keep it looking its best all year. Shrubs with berries, such as viburnum or cotoneaster, brighten a winter day. Variety of textures also adds interest. The shiny, prickly leaves of holly next to the dull, needle-like foliage of arborvitae or yew creates an interesting apposition. Low evergreen edging around a flower bed will make a green frame summer and winter. When the perennials or annuals in the bed have finished their display, the tidy green edge will keep the garden looking inhabited.

THE KITCHEN DOOR

I N many houses, family and close friends use the kitchen door exclusively. If the kitchen door leads straight off the parking area, that door is the most convenient for general use. Groceries can be carried straight to where they belong, and muddy or wet shoes won't damage carpeting or a wooden floor. And this arrangement is comfortable because the kitchen is a friendly gathering place in most homes.

Indeed, many houses are so totally oriented to the kitchen that the front door is never used. The drive, fences, and parking are arranged so that even a

Generous front porches, once the summer living rooms of America,
provide architectural settings for plants. The arches of a Victorian porch,
above left, are enhanced by the repetition of hanging baskets of begonias.
The bright flowers of annuals and perennials, above, can be enjoyed from
the porch. The patina of paint and time gives this Santa Fe door, left,
character. A few self-seeded hollyhocks herald summer.

stranger arriving for the first time wouldn't make the mistake of trying to enter at the front. The unused door may be stuck shut, or people inside may not be sure how to open it.

If the kitchen entrance is the preferred way in and out of your house, make the most of it. If it is now simply a small door on the side of the house, adding a porch or at least a small porch roof will enhance the entrance. Lights on either side of the door will make it welcoming at night. Widening the steps can make the door more important visually and provide a place to sit while shucking corn or shelling peas on a summer evening. If there is sun, the kitchen door is the perfect place to have an herb garden or a decorative vegetable garden along the lines of an English cottage garden, with vegetables and flowers growing together. The garden need not be large. A path with plants flanking it and perhaps a small shrub on one side of the door will create a mood of welcome. A kitchen garden should be casual and friendly. You and your family will enjoy the many trips in and out of the kitchen door if you get to walk through a garden each time.

THE FRONT DOOR

I F the kitchen door is the one you use most, and you have made an effort to create a garden and a welcoming atmosphere there, what happens to the front door? Even if the door is not actively used, the landscaping at the front door affects the appearance of the house, particularly from the street. The front door and front porch, if there is one, are usually the architectural centerpiece of the house façade. Whether or not this entrance is frequently used, it should have proper lighting, plants in scale to the door size, and a place for people to stand before they go in.

When the front door is the usual entrance, you should certainly consider a garden to beautify that area. Paths and the walls of the house provide the structural backbone, with flower beds and shrubs on both sides of the front path. You can make the beds in interesting shapes—triangles or squares alternating with paving, or, if there is substantial paving at the entrance, you can make a planting bed by removing some of the stone or brick. A low wall or fence extending out from a wall of the house can create a courtyard enclosure that is separate from the rest of the landscape.

In an urban setting the mood at the front entrance is usually more formal and structured. Carefully shaped topiaries, neatly clipped hedges, and elegant planters are called for. It is especially important to have some evergreen shrubs with a dense growth habit. Such plants function as green architecture; they help soften the vertical planes of the house front without concealing the architectural details. On the entrance porch of an elegant townhouse, for instance, a pair of large planters of terra cotta or of wood painted black or dark green, displaying juniper in a clipped vertical spiral or a tight ball of holly or box on a tall stem, adds a luxurious note.

The steps leading to the high porch of a Victorian house may be flanked by tight balls or cones of yew. Holly can also be clipped into tight shapes. Variegated holly will add sparkle and color, as will the red berries in winter. Some plants, such as yucca, hebe, or cactus, which have dramatic and stylized forms, make architectural statements on their own. These too, will create pizzazz at the front door. Cheerful color can be added seasonally in pots or in plantings between permanent shrubs.

THE FRONT PORCH

A large porch across the front of a house is the architectural equivalent of apple pie in the United States. The porch was the social hub of many homes in the summer until television, air conditioning, and traffic drove people into the house or back yard. Occupied or not, the porch is still there, a large architectural space that can be dreary with no furnishings. The front-door welcome at a house with a big porch can be enhanced by pots, perhaps hanging plants, and a coat of paint. The porch may have its own decorating scheme, with the floor painted dark green or gray, white trim on posts and railings, and the ceiling pale blue for lightness. A few pieces of outdoor furniture, such as a teak bench, a wicker chaise longue or rocker, a porch swing or glider, complete the look. If you have a big porch, treat it as a room even if you don't use it for sitting and rocking. The furnishings will make the front of your house look gracious.

CHAPTER

4

A PUBLIC
OR PRIVATE
FRONT YARD?

A beautifully designed and executed brick wall topped by pickets and posts ensures privacy for a front garden. The gate and arch provide a hospitable view into the garden, an invitation to enter rather than a barrier.

*I*N southern California real estate jargon, a house with an eye-catching front yard has "curb appeal." Before you redesign your front property, decide whether you want it to have curb appeal, with gardens for those passing by to see, or whether you prefer a *hortus conclusus,* a garden enclosed by a hedge or fence for intimacy and privacy.

Aesthetic or practical reasons may make it necessary to surround the front yard. Aesthetic concerns include the need for vertical planes, which either fencing or hedging can provide, to contrast with flat terrain or variety of texture and color; the desire to block an unat-tractive view; to create a "room" that acts as a transition between the house and driveway; or simply to provide a backdrop for a garden. A classic exam-ple of such a backdrop is a wall or an evergreen hedge planted as a foil for the shapes and colors of a perennial border.

Practical reasons for enclosing a front yard include the need to keep children or dogs at home, to fence a swimming pool for safety, to block traffic noise from the street, or to create privacy. In areas where wind is a con-stant factor, such as near the ocean or on a prairie, enclosure is a necessity to protect plants from desiccating winds. A high hedge or fence will also keep snow from drifting and wind and rain from buffeting the house in all seasons.

Whether the front yard is to be pub-lic and on display or private and en-closed, it should be a beautiful space, a world that gives pleasure to the home-owner and visitors year-round. A suc-cessful plan will incorporate the diverse components into a pleasing and practi-cal composition. Whether the front landscape is a spirited display or a con-templative retreat, it presents endless opportunities for gardening.

· The Front Yard on Display ·

A N open front yard with colorful, dec-orative gardens for all to see is a new trend in American landscaping. As peo-ple look for more space for garden making, they are reclaiming the front yard. Front display gardens often go right out to the sidewalk, and may even jump across the sidewalk into the tree pit area. Back yards, often crowded with large shade trees and the accoutre-ments of outdoor living, such as a swimming pool and a deck for picnics and barbecues, no longer have room for gardens. Then the front becomes the perfect forum for displaying your hor-ticultural talents. Gardeners are usually generous folk, happy to share informa-tion, knowledge, seeds, and plants. The same generosity may encourage them to share the pleasures of a beautiful garden with neighbors and people pass-ing by.

DECORATIVE GARDENS OF VEGETABLES, FLOWERS, OR GRASSES

W H A T kind of garden suits the front best? People who decide to have a front

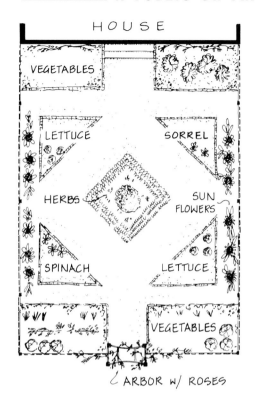
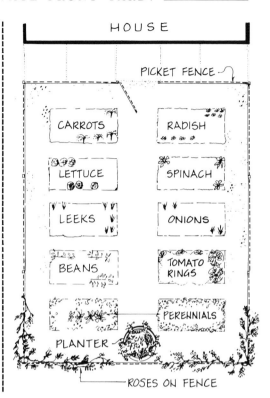

When the front yard is the only place for vegetables and flowers, create an enclosed garden with an interesting geometric pattern.

garden seem to be fairly uninhibited about their choices. Gardens featuring flowers, grasses, or vegetables are seen more and more. If the front yard has a full day of sun, a vegetable garden is a practical idea. It is easy to lose enthusiasm for a vegetable garden stuck out of sight in the back yard. If it is in the front for all to see, garden pride will keep the gardener on his toes weeding and harvesting. Giving a front vegetable garden a definite structure, with a wide central path, attractive fencing, and a gate with a vine-covered arbor over it, will make it a pleasure to look at. Vegetables arranged in careful patterns are as pleasing as other plants. It is the imaginative display that is important.

Garden historian Leslie Close turned the front of her Long Island property into a large vegetable garden three years ago for aesthetic reasons. "I thought it would look nice," she says.

Front yard flower displays are a gift to the neighborhood. Strollers at the lake front, top, enjoy summer perennials. An elegant city garden, above, is an oasis. Ryan Gainey's front garden, above right, spills over to the street. Bright field flowers suit the simple lines of a cottage, below right.

The 100-by-110-foot area is enclosed on two sides by the house and a studio, which provide structure and protect the garden from the constant seaside wind. The two remaining sides are bordered by fencing fronted by raspberries, blueberries, and roses. The center path, in line with the front door, is a wide boardwalk, and the mood of the house, path, and garden is informal. "The garden is fun," says Close. "We grow what we like to eat, and the garden changes every year."

A strong design for beds and paths is important when planting an edible garden in front. The structure of the garden will keep the area interesting even in winter when no vegetables are growing. One effective plan is to have a series of beds measuring about 3 feet by 5 feet laid out in a pattern. The garden will consist of one or two rows of rectangles. The plants don't have to be in straight lines; each rectangle can be closely planted with a single vegetable. The lacy foliage of carrots, tight clumps of red or green lettuce, the huge leaves and red stems of rhubarb or red-stemmed Swiss chard are decorative and make interesting massed plantings. Tomatoes are rangy, but if planted in tomato rings, placed in a line, they won't flop over and look messy.

Other plants can be added to the front vegetable garden, too. Many herbs are well mannered and can be appropriately included as edging if they are small, like parsley or thyme, or planted in a central geometric bed. Flowers such as sweet peas, which can't be grown in the flower garden because of their need for support, would be a good addition here, too. Sunflowers, too tall for flower beds, look exuberant in a vegetable patch. Flowers grown just for cutting are a real luxury, but if you plant them in your vegetable garden, you won't rob other parts of the garden for bouquets. A combination vegetable/flower garden requires a big space and an interesting design. You might try planting flowers around the perimeter of the garden to dress it up. Or you could plant large masses of flowers to balance each other at either end of the garden.

A ROMANTIC ORCHARD AND MEADOW

I N rural areas, turning the front yard into an orchard with a meadow planted as groundcover makes a nostalgic land-

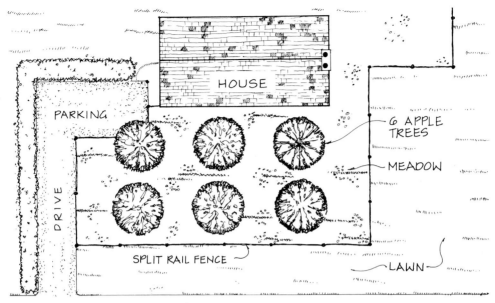

HOUSE

PARKING

DRIVE

6 APPLE TREES

MEADOW

SPLIT RAIL FENCE

LAWN

STREET & SIDEWALK

A small orchard of six trees in a meadow surrounded by a split rail fence is a romantic front yard landscape reminiscent of bygone days on the farm.

scape, reminiscent of the family farms of earlier days. Clouds of apple blossoms in the spring, followed by fruit in late summer, are enchanting. An orchard is an excellent solution for an uneven hillside at the front of the house. Since the trees are permanent, and the grass needs only rough mowing several times a season instead of weekly, the difficulties of caring for a hillside site are lessened. When planting an orchard, set the trees in rows so that the repetition of the trunks creates a pattern. Proper spacing is important so branches don't touch each other when mature. In time, fruit trees grow

into gnarled and twisted shapes, which adds further interest to the landscape. It isn't necessary to plant a great many trees; six or eight of one variety will convey the sense of an orchard. And if your property is small, you can plant semidwarf or dwarf trees to keep the orchard in scale with your lot.

If the idea of a yard full of apple trees is appealing, be aware that a fruit orchard is not a low-maintenance proposition. The tops of trees should be pruned annually so the fruit can be reached and so the top branches don't shade out lower ones. To keep the fruit large and attractive, you must spray for

Two front yard gardens that are consistent with their locale. The severity
of the desert is echoed in the sparse planting and simple lines of the
house, right. George Radford's garden in Victoria, British Columbia,
above, complements the Victorian spirit of the house with its lush
plantings of lavender, artemisia, stachys, and a potted dracaena.

various diseases several times a season. If you want to avoid pesticides, use dormant oil sprays in the spring to smother the eggs of pests. Keeping the ground free of fallen fruit will discourage animal pests too. To maintain vigor, trees should be fertilized each spring. The grass under the trees can be mowed or left rough. A mowed lawn will be tidier looking than grass cut just a few times a season, but rough grass gives a more rustic effect. While it would be wonderful to have the orchard in a meadow filled with wildflowers, competition between flowers and grass is a constant battle, with grass usually winning.

To make a wildflower meadow, you must first kill the existing grass with a herbicide or remove it by cutting the sod away, because flowers cannot get established if they must compete with tenacious grass roots. Generally a combination of annual and perennial wildflower seed is planted, with annuals providing color the first year, followed by perennials the next year. Some nurserymen advocate putting in perennial plants instead of seed to get a head start on the grass, which will eventually reestablish itself.

If you choose not to employ such intensive gardening measures, an orchard in a meadow can be beautiful and romantic even without a crop of fruit and a carpet of flowers underneath. You may appreciate having rows of ornamental fruit trees such as crabapples or flowering cherries in grass without the labor involved in achieving perfect fruit and masses of wildflowers.

AN ORNAMENTAL GRASS GARDEN

T H E recent popularity of ornamental grasses has led to some exciting experiments with grass gardens in the front yard. Oehme, van Sweden and Associates, a landscape architecture firm in Washington, D.C., has led the way in using grasses as front yard plantings. Jim van Sweden says, "The great thing about grasses is their dynamic quality. We like to think of the dimension of time. Grasses change from season to season and are effective all year long. We move taller material that has traditionally been stacked up against the foundation of the house to the edge of the property, next to the curb, which gives privacy from the street."

In cold-weather locations the dramatic tan shapes and rustling sounds of dry grasses provide an interesting addition to the winter scene. Tall grasses, such as calamagrostis or the numerous varieties of miscanthus, which grow to 5 or 6 feet, provide screening between the house and the street. Grasses are effective when planted in masses of one variety or in arrangements of various sizes, colors, and habits. Some designers have used calamagrostis to create the effect of a wheat field in the front garden. Several miscanthus plants or, in the South, cortaderia make an impressive mass after a few years. A group of _Miscanthus sinensis_ 'Gracillimus', with its arching habit and large white plumes in late summer, planted with _Panicum virgatum,_ a slender, vertical grass with delicate greenish inflorescences, and _Pennisetum alopecuroides,_ compact with arching pink blooms, makes an exciting garden. Small-scale grasses with lots of impact include the blue-foliaged _Helictotrichon sempervirens_ and the very red _Imperata cylindrica_ var. _rubra_ 'Red Baron'. An ornamental grass garden is a lively one, and the shape of the bed should be a swooping, curving arc, to emphasize the excitement of the plants.

FOUNDATIONS: TO PLANT OR NOT TO PLANT?

I N the last fifty years Americans have generally limited gardening at the front of the house to foundation planting, and permanent clumps of shrubs and trees. Evergreen shrubs such as yew and rhododendron are lined up along the base of the house to hide the foundation. For large houses built at the turn of the century, such plantings are in scale with the house, but with newer, smaller houses the proportion of plants to house has become unbalanced. At a modest ranch house, for example, a 5-foot-high shrub appears to reach halfway up the house, partially obscuring windows and giving the front an uncared-for appearance. Smaller houses need an alternative to foundation planting.

Many architects designing residences today have done away with foundation plantings. Hugh Newell Jacobson, an architect practicing in Washington, D.C., designs houses that stand alone in the landscape. The lawn runs right up to the foundation, which has been elegantly designed so that it doesn't need to be concealed. The house is an

architectural entity, and, harking back to traditions both American and European, the plantings are well removed from it.

If you are installing a decorative garden in your front yard, consider eliminating the distraction of foundation planting. If the house sits alone as an architectural unit, a garden in front of it will become more important visually. If the foundation is ugly, simplify the planting by using one or two varieties of low evergreen shrubs. These will become a green band, hiding the foundation and settling the house into the land around it.

AN OPEN FRONT WITH PRIVACY ENCLOSURE

I F the front yard garden is designed to be seen from the street, a small enclosure at the front door can provide some privacy, if that is important. You may want to get your mail or newspaper in the morning without the whole neighborhood seeing you in your slippers. Trellising or a slatted fence will allow light in and keep views from the street out. A low hedge or fence surrounding a small terraced area at the foot of the steps will give you psychological privacy, though not total concealment.

Interesting alternatives of lawn and foundation planting: Cerastium
tomentosum, *left, is a dense groundcover with prolific blossoms. Clumps
of miscanthus and pennisetum, top, are planted with perennials.
Bouteloua and coleus, above, make an exotic summer combination.*

· Enclosures: Hedges and Fences ·

IF you decide on an enclosed front yard, the purpose of the enclosure will dictate the height and the appropriate material. If the purpose is privacy, a 6- to 8-foot-high fence or hedge probably will be necessary. If the enclosure is intended to keep dogs or children in, or to make a distinction between a parking area and an entryway, a 3-foot-high fence or hedge should be adequate. Function, cost, and suitable style are the basic considerations for determining what the enclosure will be made of.

Most American homeowners enclose their properties with shrubs and trees rather than walls or fences. The choice is generally based on expense—the initial cost of planting shrubs is much less than that of building a fence or wall. However, yearly maintenance can add up. If you pay someone to clip a hedge several times a year, over twenty-five years you have made a significant investment in the hedge. A wall of brick or stone, on the other hand, requires a large initial investment, but in twenty-five years the only maintenance

it will need is repointing once, if mortar has been used. If it is a dry wall, winter weather may cause heaving, which could move some stones. However, the dry stone walls crisscrossing Pennsylvania and New England, even those that have been abandoned, have remained standing for more than a hundred years. The cost of building and maintaining a fence falls between that of hedging and stone walls. A wood fence will hold up for about fifteen years. If it is painted, the cost of repainting every five years should be considered as part of the expense. Most houses in the United States are built of wood, and from an aesthetic point of view, repeating the material of the house creates a pleasing effect.

Though in the long run the expense of maintaining a clipped hedge can be considerable in terms of time or money, in our peripatetic society we don't expect to stay in the same house for a lifetime, so we aren't usually willing to make an investment in brick or stone. And it is easier for most of us to come up with the money for hedge trimming each year than it is to make a large one-time investment in a wall.

HEDGEROWS

T H E least expensive type of hedge to maintain is a loose, natural one, in the style of a hedgerow. A hedgerow looks as though it has occurred naturally, though of course it hasn't. A mixture of varieties of shrubs should grow together to form a thicket that requires no clipping. To achieve instant privacy you may initially plant more shrubs and trees than you will need in the long run, and in ten years some overcrowded plants may have to be removed to allow room for the remaining plants to keep growing. A hedgerow planting should include fast-growing shrubs such as forsythia or weigela for quick coverage.

A hedgerow of several kinds of shrubs has an informal, almost wild look. To be most effective, it should incorporate a variety of evergreens, such as yew, holly, and juniper for solidity. Vertical or conical shapes are important as accents among the more usual rounded shrubs. Variety of leaf texture and color is important, too. Flowering shrubs chosen to bloom in sequence will provide color during the growing season. Starting with witch hazel in early spring and continuing through late summer with rose-of-Sharon and lespedeza, color will be an important component of the border. Viburnums and rugosa roses, which have flowers in spring and ornamental fruit or colorful foliage in the fall, extend the season of interest. *Euonymus alata,* also known as burning bush, has bright red leaves in autumn, as well as interesting, corky branches in winter. Many maples, both large and small, have striking fall color; so do some azaleas, such as *Rhododendron schlippenbachii* and *R. vaseyi.* A hedgerow is a good place to let bulbs naturalize, too. Masses of long-lived bulbs such as crocus or daffodils can be planted in drifts at the edge of the shrub border; the fading foliage of daffodils in early summer won't be noticed among the many other plants.

At first glance, planning such a loose border may seem quite simple. However, it is not enough to gather a variety of flowering shrubs and line them up. The whole group should be an artistic study in texture, color, and mass. By repeating a few basic plants in large

A boxwood hedge, above, makes a green border between the masonry walk and the brick walls of the house. A privet hedge at the property line, right, is a green wall separating the sidewalk from the front yard.

groups you can avoid a spotty look. To have coherence, the plants should be grouped by association, and not be a random selection. For example, rugosa roses, juniper, cotoneaster, and viburnum are adapted to the conditions of a windy, dry seaside garden and are an appropriate grouping. Rhododendrons and azaleas should not be included with these seaside plants. They belong in a woodsy situation where the soil is acid, grouped with other ericaceous plants such as leucothoe and perhaps underplanted with wildflowers and ferns.

A mixed hedgerow border is most suitable to an informal house in a rural or suburban area and should be far enough away from the house so that it doesn't appear to be swallowing it up. Such a border is not appropriate for a very small property, for when shrubs are arranged in irregular groups, they fill out as masses 10 to 14 feet wide. An informal hedgerow planted to screen the front of the house indicates that the rest of the property is also casual.

If a fence is required in addition to the screening provided by loose hedging, a sturdy, utilitarian material such as chain link or turkey wire can be in-

stalled before the border is planted. Shrubs planted on both sides of the fence will hide it completely in a short time.

CLIPPED HEDGES

A linear clipped hedge of one shrub variety creates an entirely different effect at the front of the property. It is architectural, making rigid planes like the walls of a room. This linear element is a wonderful counterpoint to the generally loose shapes of plants. A clipped hedge is suitable to any style house, though some plants may look more formal than others. Privet, which is twiggy, dense, and deciduous, looks informal, though it can be clipped into very strict shapes. Fine-foliaged, evergreen yew and boxwood look refined when properly trimmed.

When choosing a plant for this type of hedge, consider whether you want it to be evergreen or deciduous and how much maintenance various shrubs require. A properly shaped deciduous hedge retains its architectural character in winter, but without leaves it may look dull. If the year-round color and

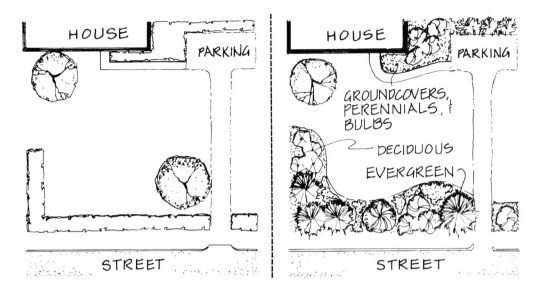

The clipped hedge, left, uses a minimal amount of space to create an enclosure. The hedgerow, right, requires less maintenance but takes up more space.

substance of an evergreen hedge suits you, consider differences in plant appearance. Yew is deep green and the needles are dull; some people find that deep color dreary. Holly, on the other hand, is deep green but shiny, so the effect is sparkling, and it has bright berries in the winter. The bright, contrasting colors of yellow-variegated holly make a very dramatic hedge. If you live in a northern climate, choices for evergreen hedges are limited to a few shrubs such as yew, spruce, and hemlock. If you are fortunate enough to live in a warm climate you have many other plants to choose from, such as laurel, oleander, and osmanthus.

FRAMING THE VIEW WITH PLANTS

I F you want to screen an unsightly view, such as a road, or frame a beautiful distant view, shrubs and trees are more versatile than fencing or walls because they can be planted in groups of different heights. Suppose that, close by a developer has put up an ugly house with a fake mansard roof covered with asphalt shingles. The new planting around the house is spindly and doesn't provide any relief. In the distance, however, may be a view of a wonderful red barn, a delight particularly on dreary, gray days. Or there may be a church steeple punctuating the

Walls and fences define space. A small shade garden opposite the front door, above left, is enclosed by lattice walls with large windows that allow glimpses into the garden. A substantial brick wall, below left, rare in American gardens, provides total privacy. A lacy iron fence, above, is a physical but not a visual barrier. Double pickets, right, are a variation on the American classic. When placed close together they ensure privacy.

sky. In this case, you could block out the offending house with a large group of evergreen shrubs and trees and leave an adjacent area open or planted with lower plants, so that the distant view will still be part of your picture.

If you are fortunate enough not to have an eyesore nearby and to have a distant view that you want to accentuate, shrubs and trees can again serve the purpose. To frame a scene, place trees or shrubs in the middle distance and on the sides, right and left, of the object of admiration. This creates a window that focuses the viewer's glance, rather than leaving the entire panorama wide open and diffusing the view.

FENCES

T W O good reasons for choosing fencing to enclose the front yard are that fences take up little space and they can be designed with pickets or rails for openness. For a property of a quarter acre or less, these are important considerations. Again, the purpose of the fence is important to consider. If it is to create privacy, a fence must be tall enough that passersby can't see over the top. Whether it is used to make a private sitting area and winter sun trap at the front entrance, to block views into a picture window, or to provide privacy for the entire front yard, the fence must be at least 6 feet tall.

If the purpose of the fence is to put the owner's stamp on a small property, separating it from the public space, it can be just 3 feet tall. A split rail or picket fence provides a wonderful place for roses or clematis to ramble. An open fence creates a public/private garden that allows views both in and out of the property. It creates a kind of psychological privacy, as distinct from visual privacy, by making a barrier through which a visitor must pass to reach the house.

A wood fence at the front of the property should reflect the architecture and style of the house, particularly if it is close to the house. A fence is an outdoor extension of the house and as such must have some visual reference to it. As often as not, a homeowner goes to the local lumber yard to find any fencing sturdy enough to keep the dog in or to comply with swimming pool zoning laws. The results look haphazard. A grape stake fence abutting the corner of a colonial house is a sorry sight. In the last five years, as awareness of and interest in gardens has grown, it has become easier to buy or build fences of varying styles. There are books that document styles, which an able carpenter can copy. Fencing companies offer models for every architectural period, including contemporary. Lattice, pickets, and board fencing, as well as finials, moldings, and gates can be put together in various combinations. The many choices are lovely, and deciding which one you want may make you feel like a child in a candy store.

Ann Masury, horticulturist at Strawbery Banke museum in Portsmouth, New Hampshire, has found records showing that the owners of houses built there in the mid-eighteenth century employed the same joiners to do interior finishing carpentry, such as stair rails and moldings, and fences. The fence repeated design elements of the house and made the land around the house belong to it. These fences were not built to maintain privacy but

to divide the front yard from the street, and the drive and barn from the rest of the property. They provided the finishing touch to a complete design.

A contemporary example of a design integrating house and fence can be seen in a design by Jeff Riley of Centerbrook Architects, in Essex, Connecticut. The 7-foot-high wood fence and entrance gate captures the space in front of the clapboard house and acts as an extension of it. "The fenced courtyard creates a sense of threshold," says Riley. "When you pass through the gate, you enter a new, special area which is quiet, where the flowers smell good, that is welcoming." The fence, painted white like the house, is built of wide, vertical slats, which allow air circulation but close off views of the house from outside.

Located on a busy suburban street, the house has tall windows that look onto the courtyard and its large, old oak and maple trees. The fenced courtyard is a necessity. It blocks views into the house from the street and creates an outdoor room, a transitional space between the house and street. The courtyard also provides a focal point

for all the public rooms of the house. Riley says, "The courtyard gives a nice focus, it unifies the house, and makes a visit to the house memorable."

Spanish-style houses in Florida and the southwestern states have preserved the wonderful tradition of courtyard entries. More architecture than horticulture, such a court is a room with the ceiling open to the sky, numerous potted plants, and possibly a small fountain or water feature. It is part house,

part garden. Tiles, both plain and brightly glazed in patterns, provide further visual excitement. Cars are parked outside the courtyard, near the street.

In the arid Southwest, as development increases the demand for a limited supply of water, garden designers are rethinking the front property. Lawns and gardens with plants that require regular watering are disappearing, replaced by native plants that need little water. Front yards are being

Two updated versions of the traditional Spanish entrance court in the Southwest. A bridge leads to wooden doors, above, punctuating a curving stucco wall. Flowing walls, left, are alive with pockets of plants. The emphatic shapes of cactus are highlighted against the simple walls.

treated more as architecture, with enclosures built for shade and larger
paved areas for parking. In sum, the
traditions of the past are pointing the
way to the future of gardening in this
demanding climate.

In such an architectural setting, each
plant is highlighted like a work of art.
One bold and dramatic cactus is as effective as a large group of softer plants.
The flower colors of indigenous plants
are often intense yellows and shocking
pinks, so large masses of plants aren't
necessary for a vivid effect. Pots are
used liberally in Spanish courtyards.
Each plant is made distinct by this
treatment, and the gardener has complete control over watering when
plants are in containers.

Wall building has not disappeared
completely from the United States. In
areas where Spanish gardens are traditional, stucco walls are still regularly
built to create privacy enclosures. But
in most parts of the country, masonry
walls made of brick or stone are pro-
hibitively expensive. A less expensive,
but happy, compromise is a combination masonry and wood fence. A 2- or
3-foot wall of fieldstone or brick topped
by a white wood fence of narrow round

pickets with posts finished with finials
makes a charming juxtaposition of materials. Such a combination wall and
fence is especially effective when there
is a change of grade and a retaining wall
is needed. The wall can be built just tall
enough to hold the earth in place, and
the fencing on top makes it taller without resorting to solid masonry.

Enclosure, whether it consists of fencing, clipped hedges, or loose hedgerows of shrubs, makes the front yard an
intimate, private world. It can shut out
noise, dust, and traffic and give homeowners their own outdoor world.

· *Bold Statements in the*
Front Yard ·

S O M E homeowners make even more
dramatic changes in the front yard by
combining permanent structures with
plants or by using the area as a setting
for family activities or works of art. The
results can be striking, but keep in
mind that placing a permanent structure in the front garden is a risky ven-
ture. Once a pond, swimming pool, or
tennis court is in place, there is no
moving it if you change your mind.

These projects require confidence and careful planning on the part of both the designer and homeowner.

The usual motivation for undertaking such bold projects is practicality. The front yard may be the only part of the property with enough space for a large construction project. In new construction on a small plot of land, putting a pool or tennis court in the back might locate the house too close to the front property line. And on steep terrain the site may dictate the location of the house and amenities.

When designers are forced to push the limits of traditional design, the results can be exciting. Homeowners with the imagination to go along with unusual design ideas will end up with an innovative, yet practical, house and landscape.

SWIMMING POOLS

T H E R E are two approaches to putting a swimming pool in the front of the property. One is to hide it behind hedging or fencing. The other is to put it on view, boldly incorporating it into the overall design of the house and landscape. The pool may look like a decorative reflecting pool, built as an extension of the house, or it may be somewhat removed, enclosed within a hedge or fence, and connected to the house visually and physically via paths, gates, and pergolas. The accessories of an enclosed pool can be hidden by a fence or hedge, attractively designed to suit the style of the house. An architectural element such as a gate and trellis relates the pool to the house. A path from a door of the house to a gate at the pool is the important link connecting the two areas.

When a pool is designed to be seen from the outside of the house, it is more than a recreational amenity, it is an important component of the landscape. It can be shimmering plane of gray or black water, with the water creating movement and light, rather than the bright aqua rectangle of 1950s pools. Sophisticated decking of stone or wood can contain the pool and relate it to the architecture of the house. If the pool is an extension of the house, the clutter of chairs and umbrellas and, in winter, the pool cover must be considered, and perhaps even banned, for these will be part of the view from the house. In cold-weather areas a snow-

*Gracious brick courtyards are traditional in
Charleston, South Carolina. Renovated recently
by Hugh and Mary Palmer Dargan, these two
enclosed garden entries combine brick, topiary,
and lush plantings for maximum impact.*

laden vinyl cover isn't an enticing view, though at a weekend or summer house, it may seem more acceptable. The convenience of having a pool close to the house where it is always visible must be balanced against the inconvenience of an unattractive view during the winter months.

When a pool is designed as an extension of the house, the line between indoors and outdoors is intentionally blurred. Cutting down the sense of separation between indoors and outdoors by the use of large expanses of glass and by extending the plane of the floor to the outside eliminates the hemmed-in feeling that the walls of a house can create. The visual and physical availability of the pool will make it seem part of the living space.

Jerry Lee, of LDA Architects in San Francisco, recently designed and built a house-terrace-pool complex in Redding, California. On this project, he says, there were several reasons for designing a compound with the pool in the front. The homeowners wanted indoor and outdoor living that would be easily accessible and on one level. Intensely hot summers meant that it was important to have shady areas at the

pool, so it was located on the north side of the house. Putting the pool elsewhere on the steep site would have required building retaining walls and building the pool on fill. The choice seemed inevitable.

The resulting design is a house with two wings that project toward the front of the property, creating a courtyard. A fence further extends the planes of the two wings. The wedge-shaped lap pool is close to the front of the property, and, says Lee, also serves as a reflecting pool.

The pool and deck are on the same level as the living room, and large glass doors make the pool area an extension of the living room. This physical connection, plus the fence, which links the two wings of the house and encloses the pool, make this project a convincing design.

Architect William Gleckman was inspired to surround the front of a house he was designing with a U-shaped pool after visiting a ninth-century palace in Bukhara that had water channels on three sides. "I knew I had to build a house surrounded by water someday," says Gleckman. The 82-foot-long U-shaped pool follows the contour of the living room wall, which extends out from the facade of the house. The edge of the pool is only a few feet from the living room, down several steps. The living room walls are oversized sliding glass doors, making the indoors and the pool area one design unit. The living room also steps down toward the pool, further enhancing the cohesiveness of the design.

The pool fencing is made of cedar-framed tempered glass panels, which are designed to be seen through. The house appears to float above the pool, swimming seems an almost secondary function of the pool. This public and somewhat ceremonial appearance is further heightened by a rounded bridge arching over the pool. The bridge creates a dramatic connection between the house entrance and a gate in the fence. On a practical level, the arched bridge allows swimmers to do laps in the Olympic-size pool.

Both of these designs with swimming pools in front confine parking and the driveway to as small an area as possible on the side of the property. The entrance used in daily living is given minimal importance on the side of the house.

TENNIS COURTS

PUTTING a tennis court on the front of a small property may seem as subtle as being greeted by an elephant at the door. It takes careful thinking and arranging to integrate a tennis court successfully into the front property. The court area (36 by 78 feet) and the standard 10-foot tall enclosure fence create a large mass. Shrubs or trees with the heft to disguise or soften the tall fences will occupy a significant amount of space, too. And the trees or shrubs should be planted far enough away from the fence so that shade and falling leaves are not problems.

Earth berms with planting on top are a popular and relatively inexpensive way to disguise a tennis court. The mounded earth appears to cut down the height of the fence, and the plants on top provide additional coverage. For stability, a berm should be built at a ratio of 3 feet of width to 1 foot of height; to build a 3-foot-high berm, you should have a 9-foot-wide base. A berm uses a lot of ground space, so on a small property it may have an effect opposite of the one intended. The berm may actually draw a viewer's attention

Privacy for outdoor living spaces. Designed by LDA Architects, San Francisco, the swimming pool courtyard, left, is closed off from the street by a textured glass fence. Glass bricks in a courtyard wall in Florida, above, allow light in and views out.

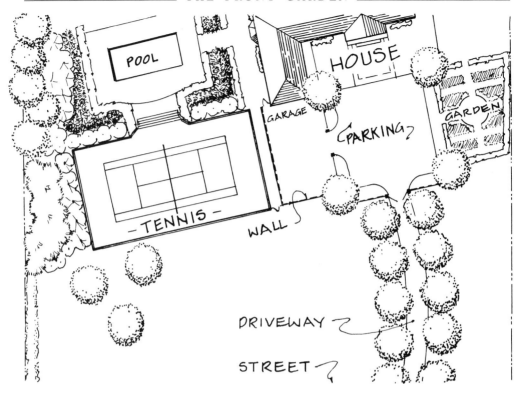

A design by Robert A.M. Stern Architects clusters the parking area, tennis court, pool, and garden around the house. Fences separate the various components.

to the tennis court instead of disguising it because it is an artificial effect.

Another way to make a tennis court less conspicuous is to excavate the site and sink the court 3 to 6 feet. The paved surface will be less visible and the fence need not be so high. Lowering the court will double or triple the cost of construction, however, for in addition to the excavation, retaining walls must be built. Or, if there is room, the land can be graded on a slope outward from the court. Layers of

gravel for drainage will also have to be installed.

On a property of less than an acre, accommodating several different outdoor functions such as a tennis court, parking, gardens, and swimming pool, requires careful planning. Whether you put these elements in front of the house or behind it, dotting them around the property reduces the already limited open space and the sense of spaciousness. The most successful designs for small properties consolidate the various built elements, so that part of the property remains open.

The architect Robert A. M. Stern came up with an ingenious arrangement on a small flag lot, which involved clustering all the built components. The house, parking court, garden, tennis court, and swimming pool are all contiguous to each other, separated yet connected by hedges and fences. One reads often of creating garden rooms, and this design literally has adjoining rooms for each function. Walls and hedges divide and enclose each room, and gates and paths are the doors and halls between them.

The house is situated asymmetrically on the lot, with the parking court directly in front. On one side of the parking court, screened by a wall with gates, is the tennis court, surrounded by a fence. Behind the tennis court and on the side of the house is the swimming pool, enclosed by layers of hedges and shrubs. In front of the house, on the other side of the parking court, is a small formal garden surrounded by hornbeam hedges.

The width of the property to the setback lines has been used to tightly group the built portions of the land-scape. This arrangement leaves most of the front and back open, with plenty of room for trees and lawn. The principle of grouping components and then separating them visually with hedges or groups of shrubs, is one that any homeowner can use.

THE FRONT YARD AS ART

I T is a fine line that separates gardening and art. In fact, Martha Schwartz, of Schwartz, Smith, Meyer Landscape Architects, based in San Francisco, argues that gardens are art, or should be: "A garden doesn't have to be background or a pleasant setting; it should have its own image and meaning."

A bagel garden once designed by Martha Schwartz in the Back Bay section of Boston would be categorized as garden art. It was an irreverent garden, but principles of symmetry and geometry so dear to French garden design were present in its design and execution. The garden was a 22-by-22 foot space, enclosed by an elegant wrought iron fence, in front of a Georgian row house. Two concentric squares of boxwood hedging reiterated the outer square of fencing and formed the struc-

When art is incorporated into a garden, plants are secondary. Martha Schwarz's design combined a traditional fence and hedge with colored gravel and painted bagels, below left. Lawrence Underhill's simple settings of pachysandra and trees highlight sculpture in a Portland garden, above left and above.

ture of the garden. The 30-inch strip between the two hedge squares was filled in with purple gravel, the kind sold in aquarium supply stores. Schwartz calls it a *petit parterre broderie,* and it did indeed recall the colored gravel used in elaborate French *broderie* gardens to emphasize patterns. The center square was planted with ageratum, the same color as the gravel.

The purple gravel also created texture and color contrast for the intensely colored bagels. Coated with brightly colored, weatherproof marine spar paint, ninety-six bagels became the "flowers," the colorful decorative elements, of the garden. Set out in strict linear arrangement, they reiterated the lines of the garden structure.

Aside from being amusing to walk by, what did this garden mean? Designer Schwartz says, "The bagel garden was intended to be humorous but also artistically serious. The irony of the garden was created by the juxtaposition of the formal geometry (imperial and elite) with the bagels (homey and domestic)." Although the garden was small in size, it will not be easily forgotten.

SCULPTURE AND VISTAS

A garden can also make an artistic statement in a more conventional way, as an environment for sculpture. A woodsy hillside property in Portland, Oregon, is home to numerous pieces of sculpture, commissioned by the homeowner from artists living in the Northwest. Many of the sculptures are placed in garden settings bordering the drive, which winds up a long hill to the house. The approach and front yard have become a series of exciting visual experiences in which sculpture is the focal point. Each area is like a stage, with sculpture, plants, sky, and water creating a constantly changing drama.

As you progress up the gravel drive, you are carried from one vista to the next. The flow of the curves gives the garden its momentum and structure. Around each curve is another surprise, a sculpture in its own setting. And the return trip down the hill reveals a different picture. The sculptures are placed so that they can be seen from various places on the property and from the house. Standing on revolving pedestals, the sculptures can be moved to alter the view. Lights high in the trees provide nighttime silhouettes and shadows, so the sculptures can be appreciated in yet another way.

This garden has been carefully nurtured for thirty years by landscape architect Lawrence Underhill. He has carefully created settings for the sculptures, watched the plants as they have grown, and moved the sculptures in and out of the garden as new pieces were commissioned or old ones given new homes. Native plants such as Douglas firs (*Pseudotsuga menziesii*) and western sword ferns (*Polystichum munitum*) form the backbone of the garden. Flowering shrubs, including hundreds of rhododendrons, ornamental cherries, and viburnums, add brightness during a long season. The few flower beds are segregated in their own areas.

Plants create settings for the sculpture and contrasts of texture, color, and form. A smooth, white marble figure of a mother holding a baby, by Don Wilson, rests in a large bed of green pachysandra next to a pond. In the same bed a low rhododendron with small, dull leaves and a dwarf Japanese maple with finely cut red foliage are highlighted against the pachysandra's low whorls of green leaves. Set off in this way the rhododendron and maple also become sculptural elements. As one moves around the garden, the backdrop for the statue shifts from water to groundcover to the red and green of shrubs.

"Canyon Passage," a tall bronze sculpture by Hilda Morris, towers above a pond on the western side of the property. The top of the sculpture seems to touch the sky, as do the jagged tops of Douglas firs in the background. The reflections of plants and sculpture in the pond make a constantly changing picture as the water goes from gray and choppy to blue and still, depending on the weather. At the end of the day the setting sun creates dramatic silhouettes of trees and sculptural forms.

Sculpture adds another dimension and further meaning to a garden. Placing a manmade solid object among the green, soft, moving shapes of plants creates instant drama. As a theme for an entrance garden, sculpture provides year-round interest by focusing our attention immediately. We don't soon forget such a garden.

CHAPTER

5

SOME SUCCESSFUL FRONT GARDENS

Rosalind Creasy's abundant garden of edibles in autumn. Always changing, the garden is cultivated all year for a succession of flowers, fruits, herbs, and vegetables. The structures are portable. Bricks are laid in sand, and the pergola is bolted together for easy removal.

So far we have looked at how American front yards and gardens have evolved and how they are changing today in a general way. Understanding why front yards look and function as they do leads to considering how they could look and work better.

In this chapter we present case studies of nine very different front yards designed by homeowners as well as professional garden designers. The case studies illustrate how unusual or difficult sites were made practical, beautiful, and suited to the needs of the homeowner.

A SHINGLED COTTAGE
ON FARMLAND NEAR THE SEA

❧

Garden Design by Mary Riley Smith

*L*ITTLE did I know, when my husband and I bought a modest colonial-style house in Sagaponack, on eastern Long Island, that my efforts to deal with the property would lead to a career in garden design. Since neither my husband nor I was a gardener, our initial concerns were with improving the looks of the house and organizing the functional aspects of the property. Soon, though, the allure of plants and flowers had us gardening, and we became engrossed in the work of planting and pruning.

The property is a long, narrow one-acre plot on the main street of an eighteenth-century farming village. The house is set back from the road on a small ridge, giving us sunset views, cool summer breezes, and swirling winter winds. Being near the sea in a flat landscape, wind is a constant element to be dealt with, and clipped privet hedges enclose many properties in this area. We are blessed with wonderful soil, "Bridgehampton loam," a gardener's dream.

Hedges planted years ago created a framework around our new property. A sheared 6-foot-high privet hedge, essential as a windbreak and for privacy, closed off the front yard from the street. On the sides of the property, loose clumps of old-fashioned deciduous shrubs, including honeysuckle, lilacs, and weigela, were well established. The driveway, along one edge of the property, was backed by an unclipped hedge of honeysuckle. We added a hedge of burning bush (*Euonymus alata*) on the other side of the driveway to screen it from the house.

When the house was built, the land at the front of the ridge was scooped away to build the foundation. Ugly cement-block retaining walls extended forward from the house to create a parking court. Even to a nongardener it was apparent that planting was desperately needed to cover those walls.

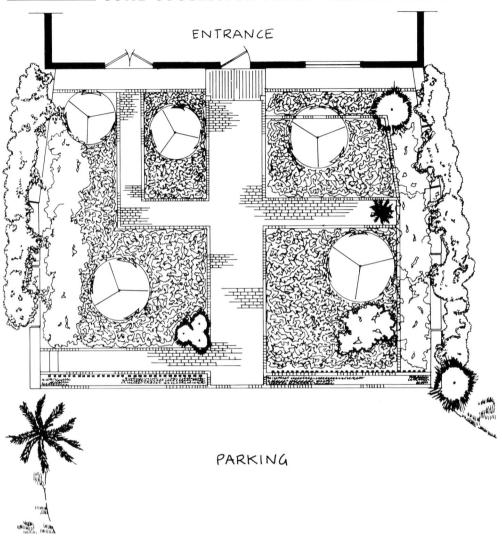

ENTRANCE

PARKING

A new garden and paths make a welcoming entrance to the house.

My first attempt at planting out the wall failed. A row of climbing euonymus died the first winter, scorched by the winter sun. During the first summer, our gardening efforts consisted mainly of picking the New Dawn roses already growing in the yard.

The second year we contracted with an architect, Clayton Morey, to remodel the kitchen and redesign the ga-

Birch trees, left, soften the tall façade of the house. A fragrant rose, Nova Zembla, graces the fence. Two views of planting, above. The color white, in the birch trees, variegated foliage, rhododendron blossoms, and fence, is the theme of the front garden.

rage doors on either side of the entrance door by the parking area. He came up with an additional proposal to make a porch roof over the entrance door, which at that point was a plain opening in the gable end of the house. With the garage doors replaced by windows, and the door enhanced by a porch, this end of the house, facing the street, looked entirely different. The porch tells a stranger arriving for the first time that this is indeed the proper way in.

There is an important lesson here in how such a small change can alter the impression and mood of a house. An entrance with architectural details, such as a roof, posts, and a porch, is inviting. In spring and summer, pots of flowers placed near the door add further embellishment.

In addition to improving the front door entrance, we had the telephone and electric wires buried. This is another nonhorticultural step that makes a big difference in the look of a house and property. Having wires drooping across the front yard is like having a clothesline out front. They are messy and are better left unseen. For a fairly modest amount of money the wires can

be buried, and I urge everyone with overhead wires to get them out of sight.

With the wires buried and a new porch roof in place, the property was beginning to look better. It became obvious that moving the car parking area would be a further improvement. A gravel parking court was placed 20 feet out from the house, which left space for a garden and a 4-foot-wide brick path between the parking area and the front door. Brick was chosen for its traditional look, in keeping with the house. A narrower path at the driveway end of the space, at a 90-degree angle to the front door path, led the way to the side and back yard. This formed two garden beds in the front of the house, each measuring 8 by 15 feet. A white picket fence was built parallel to the house to separate the garden from the parking court. Without setting out to do so, we had created the basic structure of a cottage garden.

The first consideration was how to soften the height of the gable end of the house, which towered over the front garden. Three groups of clump birch, chosen for their lacy foliage and slender habit, were placed in the front garden beds. The trees would not block out light from inside the house, and they made the front façade less severe.

Then we made another attempt to cover the cement block walls with plants. Ivy was planted at the base of the wall, and this time it took. We placed several kinds of shrubs with year-round interest in front of the walls to hide them and to provide a backdrop for smaller plants. The New Dawn roses planted at the top of the walls twenty-five years ago now tumble down into the garden, and the shrubs below reach up toward the roses. *Rhododendron chionoides*, a small variety with white flowers, rockspray cotoneaster (*Cotoneaster horizontalis*), inkberry (*Ilex glabra*), and Tartarian dogwood (*Cornus alba* 'Elegantissima'), with red twigs in winter and variegated foliage in summer, form the background planting.

A blue false cypress (*Chamaecyparis Lawsoniana*) creates a vertical accent in one corner near the house. Two small clumps of juniper provide winter interest, and a large clump of barberry (*Berberis thunbergii* 'Rose Glow') provides color most of the year. In spring, old-fashioned flowers such as daffodils, single white peonies, white foxgloves, and bleeding heart flourish in front of the shrubs. In summer my garden includes bright flowers like achillea, *Sedum* 'Autumn Joy', artemisia, and *Heuchera* 'Palace Purple'. Two large clumps of a variegated grass, *Phalaris canariensis*, add a contemporary touch.

A successful cottage garden is more than a gathering of old-fashioned plants. It must have structure, which in this case is provided by walls, paths, and the white picket fence. A theme, such as a strict color scheme or groups of plants from one family, will also unify a cottage garden. I have used plants with wine-colored foliage, which is a pleasing contrast to the sand-colored paint of the house, with white for extra sparkle, as a general color scheme. Groups of berberis and heuchera carry out this motif, and many of the flowers are white. White is also repeated in the variegated foliage of grasses, shrubs, and a few hostas.

A garden at the front door creates a welcoming entrance for friends and family. And it forces the gardener to become a better gardener. If you care about plants, it is impossible to walk by a weed or dead flower several times a day without flicking it away.

A PERENNIAL GARDEN
IN VANCOUVER

❧

Joel and Joan Brink

*T*H E need for sun and open space to plant flowers inspired Joan Brink to turn the south-facing front yard of her Vancouver house into an abundant perennial garden. "The back garden is a typical woodsy Northwest garden shaded by several cedar trees. Rhododendrons, ferns, and wildflowers thrive there. The flower gardens in the front got larger as I collected more plants," says Joan.

The garden beds line the front path and trace the perimeter of a small lawn on one side of the front yard, which measures 50 by 50 feet. Architecture is an important component in creating an attractive garden, and the tall, gray-and-white shingled house with high, dark gray steps to the porch provides a

A path and white picket fence provide structure for the Brinks' profuse perennial garden.

perfect backdrop for the perennials. Pots with topiary and seasonal flowers sit on the steps. The lower half of the house is softened by a huge wisteria.

The front of the property was recently given a white fence, which pulled the garden together visually, according to Joan. "It gave it a frame, which a small garden really needs. It made it complete." The fence keeps dogs and children from wandering through and gives further structure to the garden. The fence design was based on traditional Nantucket fences, which often have a wood strip finishing the top rather than open pickets. "I carried a piece of molding back from Nantucket so I could have the fence copied," she said.

The front garden had been in place for a number of years, but five years ago the Brinks started energetically removing lawn and expanding the flower beds. It was to be an English perennial garden, and Joan read every book she could find on the subject. The damp, sometimes overcast weather of the Vancouver area is often compared to the weather in England. The difference is the dry summers. "Some summers we have to water a lot," says Joan. Still, the temperate climate and abundant flower garden are reminiscent of England.

Both Joan and Joel work on the garden, but Joan is the plant collector. She favors perennial geraniums and campanulas and has several varieties of each. The current star of the garden is a shrub, *Romneya coulteri,* which took several years to find. Its white flowers with 6-inch crepelike petals in the spring sound a luxuriant note at the front gate. Traditional perennials, such as bearded iris, foxglove (*Digitalis mertonensis*), dame's rocket (*Hesperis matronalis*), lupine (*Lupinus*), Welsh poppy (*Meconopsis cambrica*), and forget-me-not (*Myosotis scorpioides*), fill the garden from spring through fall. There are several roses, the most dramatic one being an old Dr. van Fleet, which got so big it pulled down the hawthorn tree it was clambering over. Annuals keep the garden full all summer.

And what of the winter garden? "I don't mind it being empty during the winter—part of the thrill of a perennial garden is the speed with which it becomes tall and luxurious. The rapid change always fascinates those who pass by," Joan explains.

The healthy soil necessary for plants

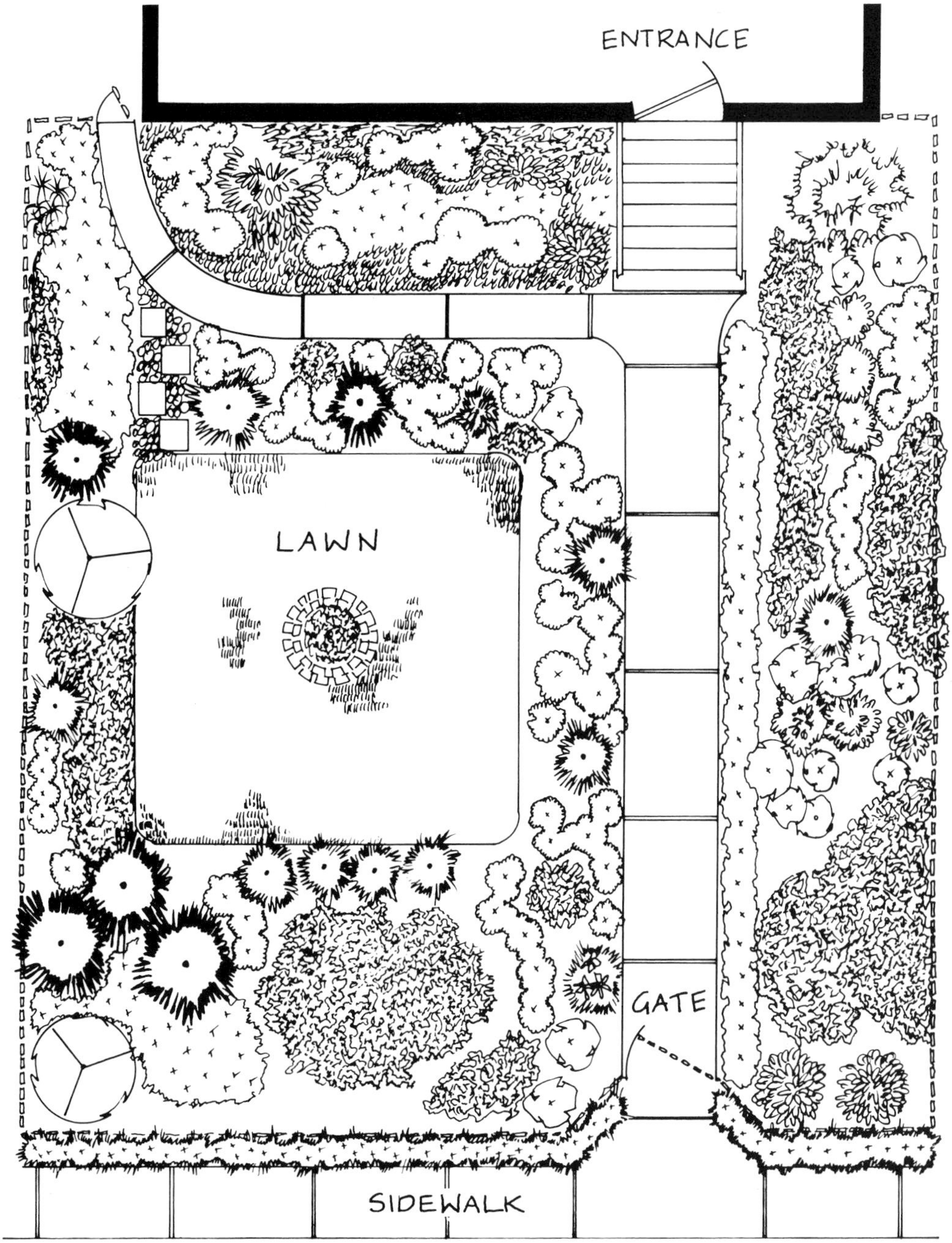

ENTRANCE

LAWN

GATE

SIDEWALK

A small front yard turned into a lush flower garden.

Several views of the spring display in the Brinks' front garden. The gray house and steps are a firm and neutral backdrop for the bright blossoms of hesperis, iris, poppies, lupine, and lychnis. Perennials that self-sow, like forget-me-not, are allowed to find their own spots throughout the garden.

to grow well is maintained by adding mushroom manure or seaweed to the garden every winter. The plants are frequently rearranged, and digging in the garden offers an opportunity to add organic matter.

People in the Brinks' Vancouver neighborhood make a point of coming by the garden to see what is currently in bloom. A beautiful front garden is a gift to people passing by. Joan says, "The garden is right out there for people to see, and you like to share it."

A WHEATFIELD
IN SUBURBAN VIRGINIA

❧

Design by Tom Mannion
with Louise Kane
of Garden Gate Landscaping, Inc.

ONE is surprised at first to see what appears to be a field of wheat instead of a lawn in front of a colonial-style house in suburban Virginia. Tom Mannion, one of the designers, explains that the garden evokes that most romantic American landscape, the farm. The design draws inspiration from aspects of rural America, both manmade and natural. Mannion speaks of the farm's symbolic place in the American consciousness, of how it is a reassuring, restorative idea. The grasses remind us of a simpler time and place.

He also draws inspiration from the pastoral landscape of the region, the softness of the Shenandoah Valley and the Appalachian Mountains and the lushness of the eastern shore of Virginia. Ideas for gardens should come from the landscapes of the region rather than from England or Japan, Mannion believes. Suburban gardens can be made to feel more rural by incorporating country plants, such as shrubby viburnums, old roses, and wheat.

To achieve that look, Mannion uses indigenous plants that feel familiar and friendly, or those that look like native plants. Exotic-looking plants are not part of Mannion's palette. The grass that is planted in a bed in the front lawn is *Calamagrostis epigejos*, which looks like the wheat growing in farm fields nearby, although it is not native. Shadblow (*Amelanchier canadensis*), winterberry (*Ilex verticillata*), and viburnum strike familiar notes, as does a large Norway maple. There are also some more common suburban plants, such as crabapples underplanted with hostas and a few azaleas. Some of these plants were in place when Mannion was called in to work on the property, and he decided to leave them.

The redesign of the front focused on making the front of the property dra-

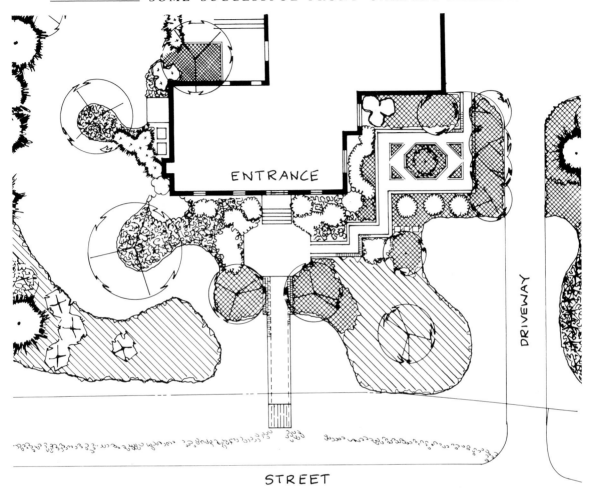

ENTRANCE

DRIVEWAY

STREET

Large areas of calamagrostis, indicated by diagonal lines, suggest a wheat field.

matic and functional. The approach to the front door was rebuilt as a wide brick path through two large areas of grass at the front of the property, then continuing on between two crabapples. "The approach feels like moving through a sequence of rooms, with the grass field as the foyer, down the hall through crabapples, to a large brick reception terrace at the foot of the steps," says Mannion. A bench on one side of the terrace offers a private place to sit even though it is on the public side of the house; it is screened from view by the tall grass near the street and the protecting branches of the crabapples.

On summer afternoons this side of the house, which faces north, is pleasantly shaded.

A zigzag path leads off the reception terrace to a separate patio and herb garden that is closed off on two sides by an ell of the house, a row of shadblows on the third side, and tall grass in the front. This 15-by-28-foot brick patio, with geometric cutouts for herbs, is the focus of the view from the dining room.

The five planting beds provide year-round interest. The center bed is a hexagon with a shrubby pink rose in the center and planted with seasonal flowers such as tulips in spring and bright annuals in summer. Last year's carefree summer display included large groups of parsley, small-leaved basil, and red begonias. Four smaller outer beds are planted with cooking and decorative herbs, including bronze fennel, com-

*Before, left, and after, above, pictures
demonstrate how a lush and romantic front
garden enhances a house. A brick terrace,
above left, at the front door doubles as an
entrance and an afternoon shade garden. The
grass garden, above, incorporates a crabapple
tree and creates the illusion of a larger yard.*

frey, rue, and lemon balm, with rhubarb for its red stems and huge leaves. The herb garden/terrace is large enough for people to gather and offers another private spot on the front property. A brick path leads from it to the driveway and parking area, which are masked by a group of shadblows.

The redesigned front yard relies on the geometry of brick paths for organization and a variety of perennials, shrubs, and trees for seasonal interest. The calamagrostis is dramatic all year. In winter the tan stalks rustle in the wind and make a light-colored mass contrasting with the brown twigginess of the deciduous plants. In early spring the grass is cut down, and while the new growth is forming, three thousand daffodils brighten the landscape. As the flowers fade and the leaves are browning and returning energy to the bulbs, newly sprouting grass covers the daffodil foliage.

The grasses used as dramatic masses in the front yard bring to mind the designs of the landscape design firm Oehme, van Sweden and Associates of Washington, D.C., which led the way ten years ago in the use of ornamental grasses. Mannion says Oehme, van Sweden's designs were definitely an influence. "They showed us how to use grasses and herbaceous perennials more boldly—they brought them out of the cutting garden," he explains. Oehme, van Sweden's example gave him the courage to make a wheat field in a front yard.

And what of the clients' reaction to the wheat field? Their original idea had been to make a Williamsburg-style garden, which they felt suited the architecture of the house. The brick patio and herb garden are a nod in that direction, but the grasses were an experiment, an act of faith in the designer. The clients agreed to try the grass as long as it would be easy to remove if they didn't like it. Several years later it is still there.

To sum up experimental front yard plantings, Mannion says, "If only more people would claim their front property for their own use, give themselves some privacy from the street, and risk some interesting, yet simple, planting schemes, my daily drive through our area would be much more pleasant. I love to drive past a well-designed front yard, and there are very few of them."

A GARDEN OF EDIBLE PLANTS

✒

Design by Rosalind Creasy

*A*S far as I'm concerned, the front yards of most American homes are wasted space," says Rosalind Creasy, the author of several books on growing and cooking unusual vegetables, herbs, and edible flowers. Creasy's front yard in California, a lush and abundant garden, a constantly changing riot of color and texture, has become her beautiful laboratory.

The front garden was turned over to intensive planting eight years ago when Creasy ran out of garden space in the back yard. To prepare for her first book, *The Complete Book of Edible Landscaping,* Creasy experimented with more and more plants. "At first," she writes, "I began sneaking edibles into the front flower bed. Finally, the whole front was dug up and turned over to annual edibles and theme gardens." In

the last eight years the front beds have included vegetable gardens with Mexican, French, Cajun, Native American, herb, salad, and oriental themes.

"The garden is designed and planted for change," she notes. Every four or five months it looks entirely different, as one crop succeeds another. "I'm on the walking and jogging route, and people are amazed at how different the garden looks in different seasons." She realized that a strong design was important to keep the many varieties of plants from looking like a hodgepodge. Structural elements such as walks, retaining walls, and trellising are important for coherence. Yet even these structural elements are made to be changed easily. The brick paths are laid in sand, and the trellises are put together with bolts, not nails, so when Creasy decides on a new arrangement, it is easily accomplished. Ornamental flowers, planted in large drifts of a few related colors, with the color scheme changing each year, also provide visual continuity.

The 3,000-square-foot garden is bounded on two sides by the paving of the driveway and front sidewalk, on the

Brick paths wind through a brilliant display of purple perilla, yellow marigolds, red salvia, and snap beans, left. Masses of ranunculus and poppies, above, cascade over the edge of the driveway.

third side by the property line, and on the fourth by the house. Most of the front is a grid of long, 3-foot-wide planting beds separated by narrow paths of brick or mulch. The eighteen beds are devoted to growing as many as seventy varieties of flowers and vegetables at any one time.

The perimeter beds are devoted largely, though not exclusively, to flowers. "As you approach the garden from the street or driveway, it should look like a plentiful cottage garden,"

SUMMER

1. celery	17. shell beans	34. runner beans
2. chicory and	18. haricots vert	35. oregano
Belgian endive	19-20. bush beans	36. tarragon
3. summer lettuces	21. shallots	37. thyme
4. strawberries	22. garlic	38. basils
5. chives	23. onions	39-40. cherry tomatoes
6. thyme	24. beets	41-43. cucumbers
7. burnet	25. carrots	44-47. tomatoes
8. sweet marjoram	26. potatoes	48. summer squash
9. zinnias and cosmos	27. flowers	49-51. melons
10. sweet corn	for drying	52. winter squash
11. winter squash	28. daylilies	53. amaranth
12. artichokes	29. hyssop and anise	54. cosmos
13. marigolds	30. lavenders	55-62. peppers
14. pole beans	31. geraniums	63-66. eggplants
15. lima beans	32. petunias	67-68. summer squashes
16. leeks	33. coreopsis	69. roselle

says Creasy, "so the outer beds are massed with flowers." A recent summer planting in a 5-by-25-foot outer bed included large groups of daylilies, iris, coreopsis, montbretia, and marguerites, with the front faced by 'Blue Perfection' violas. In the center of the bed was a large cluster of ornamental kale and cabbages. The nearby trellis entrance was covered in sweet peas. A year late the same bed had entirely new plants, except for one group of the daylilies. The kale and cabbages were replaced by flowers, including cosmos, zinnias, petunias, rose and lemon geraniums, lavender, and a large clump of hyssop. The trellis was covered with three varieties of runner beans.

Plantings in the vegetable and herb beds in the center of the garden change as dramatically as those in the outer flower beds. A vegetable bed, planted one year with marigolds, pole beans, lima beans, leeks, shell beans, small

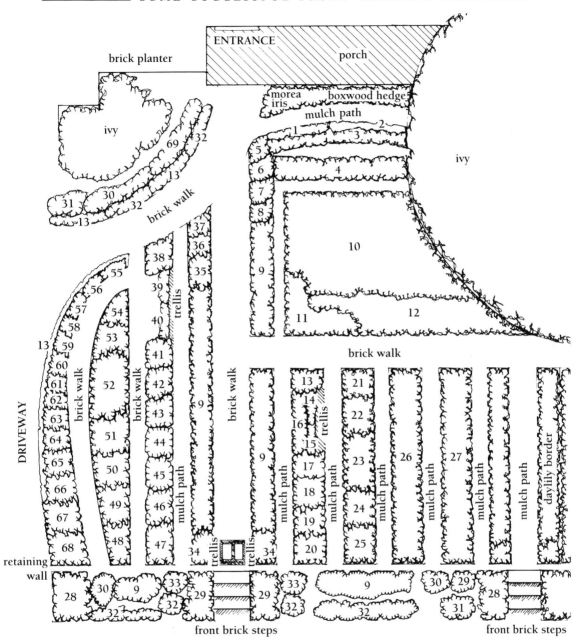

More than sixty-five plant varieties are included in Creasy's summer planting.

Rosalind Creasy's concern with the underlying structure of her garden is seen in the use of paths, trellis, steps, and arbors. These architectural elements are the foil for the loose, flowing shapes of plants. Without structure the garden could be an incoherent mass of plants.

French beans, and two varieties of bush beans, was planted the next year with radicchio, kale, kohlrabi, peas, three kinds of beets, three varieties of carrots, and calendula. Creasy likes to interplant crops such as carrots and beets with low flowering plants that can take some shade, such as violas or lobelia.

When the vegetables are harvested, the loose, low flowers cover the empty spots.

Indeed, aesthetics are the overriding concern in this garden. "I manage vegetables in my garden the way you would flowers in an ornamental garden," Creasy says. Tomatoes are tied unobtrusively to dark green trellises, and the tops are pinched so they don't get rangy and flop over. Flowers cover the earth under the tomatoes, too. Creasy won't tolerate ragged foliage and does not plant some vegetables that are subject to pests. "I don't spray pests,

and I do without the few vegetables which are a constant problem. I don't grow radishes because beetles leave the foliage looking ratty."

Such intensive planting requires constant soil amendments. When the garden was installed, the raised beds, 4 inches above the soil level, were double dug with manure. Now every time Creasy removes a crop she adds several inches of compost to the bed. She composts her own garden cuttings as well as that of several neighbors to maintain an adequate supply.

Asked how she manages harvesting the vast amount of vegetables, herbs, and flowers, Creasy explains that friends and neighbors benefit from her generosity. If a neighbor is having a party, she provides flowers to decorate the house as well as several varieties of lettuce and some nasturtium leaves and flowers for the salad. If a friend is sick, she sends over a favorite delicate vegetable. Rose petals are used to flavor sorbet, violets are candied, and herbs are dried. Managing the garden is a constant process of digging, planting, harvesting, and sharing. "The garden is my glory," Creasy says.

PRIVACY FOR TWO HOUSES
IN MASSACHUSETTS

🌿

Design by Child Associates

W H E N called upon to update two urban front gardens in Cambridge, Massachusetts, Child Associates came up with solutions that created structure and seclusion in densely built city neighborhoods. Both assignments presented similar problems. The large old houses on small lots were built close to the street, with little privacy in the front. This part of the property did allow for parking, paths, and steps, but it was all open. Windows in living and dining rooms facing the street were exposed, and the views were of the sidewalk, street, and cars. Though the two houses were of different architectural styles, one a nineteenth-century shingle house, the other a 1910 Tudor, they had similar problems of sloping sites with little private outdoor space for gardening and recreation.

The problems of exposure and lack of privacy were resolved by installing buffers of trees, shrubs, and groundcovers at the front property line. Hedging or fencing was rejected because it would shut out the rest of the neighborhood; also the strict lines of a clipped hedge or fence appear to diminish the size of a small property by indicating exactly where it stops. Instead, clumps of plants were used to mask the property line, block views into the houses from the street, and give the illusion of a parklike setting from inside.

At the shingle house the designers created privacy and enclosure by building a linear garden with an interior walk parallel to the street. The garden and walk, extending from the parking court to the property line, seem to widen the property, and create a privacy screen from the sidewalk and a connection to a private terrace and lawn on the side of the house. The herringbone-patterned brick path acts as a narrow extension of the open brick parking court. The path is punctuated at each end by sitting areas, one a circle planted in the center with the shiny evergreen foliage of European ginger (*Asarum europaeum*), the other a 10-

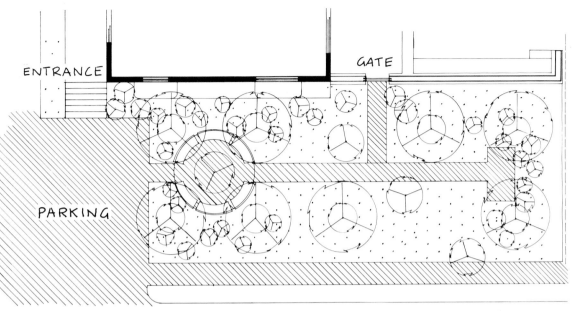

ENTRANCE GATE

PARKING

SIDEWALK

*Dense plantings of Japanese maples and woodland shrubs make a privacy buffer for
the front of the house. The dots represent 253 andromedas.*

foot-wide rectangle. A smaller path leads off the main path, through a gate in a shingled wall, to a private terrace and lawn.

The new front garden is a heavily planted, formalized woodland, 26 by 70 feet, with a 4-foot-wide path in the center. A small forest of eight Japanese maples (*Acer palmatum*) is densely underplanted with 253 andromeda (*Pieris floribunda*) as groundcover. Loose groups of Japanese holly (*Ilex crenata*) at the two long ends of the garden provide a contrast of finer, deep green foliage, and several mountain laurels

(*Kalmia latifolia*) continue the woodsy theme.

If one looks out the living room and dining room windows on the new garden, the view now is of a brick path passing through a grove of irregular tree trunks. A mood of lushness and mystery is created by the lavish underplanting of shrubs and the shady path leading to various destinations.

The second house is in the Tudor style, is very large and sits slightly to one side of the small, sloping lot, back a bit from the street. The land behind the house is a steep ravine that is not

A shady and mysterious vista, right, seen from the parking area. Details make a small garden interesting. Bricks laid in three patterns, the volume of the circle among rectangular paths, and plants chosen for variety of leaf size and texture make a complex picture. A gate, above, leads to an enclosed side garden.

suitable for outdoor living. There was virtually no outdoor sitting space in front or in back. The job here was to create some private outdoor space and to make the house appear to be more in scale with the site. The front yard and one side presented the only possible space for gardens, paths, and lawns.

Making an asset out of a difficult site, Child Associates designed an extensive series of stone retaining walls at the front and side of the house to level the land. The walls are of flat-cut Connecticut shale capped with purple bluestone to match the color of the slate roof. Purple bluestone is also used on the terraces and paths.

Tiers of American holly (*Ilex opaca*) and star magnolia (*Magnolia tomentosa*) have the dual function of seeming to diminish the towering façade of the house and providing privacy from the street. The driveway, located on one side of the house, descends from the street to a carport on the basement level. Where the driveway joins the street, a 12-foot-wide path leads to the front door.

Two long horizontal steps near the sidewalk mark the first change of level and delineate the threshold of the garden. To the right of the path, where the property is wide, new retaining walls have raised it above the level of the street; this change eliminates the view of the street from inside and makes a flat plane for a lawn and privacy planting on the perimeter. To the left of the path, and parallel to it, a retaining wall runs from the house all the way to the street. The ground slopes down steeply and acts as a buffer between the retaining wall and the driveway below.

The front of the property is screened with dense plantings of mixed evergreen trees and shrubs. Plants in loose groups, rather than hedges or fences, were used to soften the property line from the inside. American holly (*Ilex opaca*) provides the evergreen framework for the privacy plantings at the front and side. The gray trunks of five star magnolias (*Magnolia tomentosa*) weave through shrub plantings of mountain laurel (*Kalmia latifolia*), azaleas, and boxwood (*Buxus sempervirens*). Berries and shiny evergreen leaves provide winter interest, and the spring blossoms of the shrubs, underplanted with periwinkle (*Vinca minor*), make a vivid display in May.

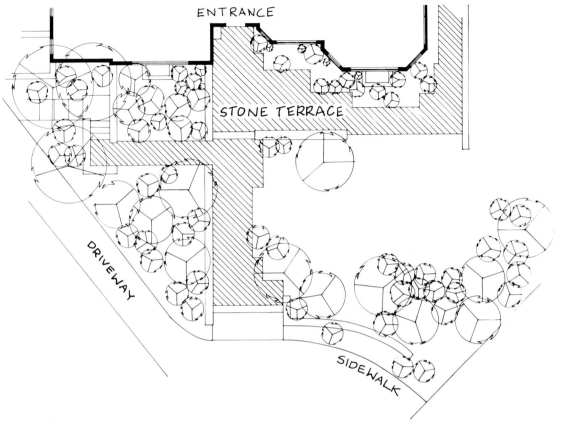

A steeply sloping front yard was terraced with retaining walls to make gardens and sitting areas. Perimeter plantings add privacy.

As the path approaches the front door, two steps mark another change of level, to the large, L-shaped bluestone terrace that adjoins the front and side of the house. The terrace, which faces south, is a year-round sitting area and on clement winter days is a protected spot to enjoy the sun. To the right of the steps and parallel to the front of the house is a 4½-foot-high, 16-foot-long privacy wall. A star magnolia planted in front of the wall adds further privacy and helps reduce the scale of the house façade.

A perennial and shrub border at the front door softens the foundation of the house and makes the entrance welcoming. In a bed with an irregular edge formed by terrace paving, autumn clematis and wisteria drape the façade of the

Two views of the front terrace and entrance. A perennial garden, clambering wisteria and ivy, and the irregular edge of the terrace add informal notes. Opposite the front door, the low stone wall and Magnolia tomentosa *provide shelter for sitting.*

house. Scilla, crocus, and narcissus cheer the garden in early spring, and old-fashioned favorites such as roses, artemesia, phlox, and asters keep it bright all summer.

The redesigned front gardens have added elegance, dignity, and practicality to these grand old houses. Privacy and intimacy were gained by reorganizing the space with architectural components. Paths and terraces act as floors for outdoor rooms surrounded by walls of trees.

A MEDITERRANEAN COURTYARD

❧

Design by Robert M. Fletcher

*I*T was a depressing ugly duckling," says Robert M. Fletcher of the house and grounds in Beverly Hills he was called upon to update several years ago. The stucco and tile Mediterranean-style tract house, built in the 1920s on a 50- by 150-foot lot with a lawn sloping to the sidewalk, had been neglected for several years. The property was ripe for a complete redesign. The new owner of the house, who was from Tuscany, wanted to evoke the mood of the Italian countryside in the small yard. The resulting design combines the strict structure of walls, steps, paths, and doors with the softness of Mediterranean plants such as olive trees.

Fletcher, a garden designer based in Los Angeles, turned the ugly duckling into a swan by painting the house and rebuilding the gardens. The first major step in the garden design was to build a 3-foot-high stucco retaining wall next to the sidewalk and backfill the area with soil so that the house and grounds were on a single level. The wall creates the first vertical plane of the front garden framework and sets off the grounds from the sidewalk.

The driveway, paved in terra cotta tiles, leads straight from the sidewalk on one side of the plot, past the house and an adjoining carport, to a garage at the back of the property. Just off the sidewalk, adjacent to the drive, is a small parking space for visitors.

Terra cotta tiles pave the major surfaces on the property, including the driveway; their earthy red color makes a visual connection between the various garden rooms. They enhance the Mediterranean mood of the house and make a beautiful foil for green and gray foliage. Terra cotta and stucco are the architectural elements that create structure and privacy in this garden.

The entrance to the house is through a garden court between the parking area and the house. The court was conceived as a spatial sequence from public to private areas, a series of enclosures leading the visitor from the street to the front door. A pair of antique Mexican doors of dark wood with massive iron hardware is the focal point of the wall separating the court from the front yard and entrance path. The contrast of stucco and wood leaves no question as to where one enters the house.

Beyond the doors the courtyard is enclosed by the living room ell of the house on one side and a garden on the other. An olive tree, one of four seen from the living room windows, is the main feature of the court, which measures 20 by 20 feet. About half of the space is given over to a wide terra cotta path. An arched loggia provides shade and shelter at the door, and a bench and numerous pots of seasonal plants are grace notes at the entry.

There is a one-step change of level from the path up to the loggia. The riser is finished with bright blue glazed tile, a striking detail that marks the step and adds a horizontal stripe of color all year. The intense blue of the tiles, the color of the California sky, is enhanced by their juxtaposition against the terra cotta pavers, a color combination

Fletcher favors. "I love the color orange against the intense blue California sky," says Fletcher of the bougainvillea 'Orange King,' which clambers up to the roof of the house from the courtyard.

The living room ell extends toward the street, dividing the front of the property into three small areas, which Fletcher treated as individual gardens. Each of the three living room windows looks at a different exposure and a different garden picture. "The living room feels as though it is in an olive grove, with each window looking into a garden with an olive tree," notes Fletcher.

And each small garden has its own distinctive design. A narrow slice of land seen from a side window is backed by an evergreen hedge of *Podocarpus gracilior*. A wall and gate separate the area from the front, and a secondary path of crushed granite passes through the garden from the front to the back of the house, circling under an olive tree that fills most of the space between the house and the rear property line. Asiatic star jasmine *(Trachelospermum jasminoides)*, a groundcover used throughout the property instead of grass, carpets this small area. The jas-

The entire front property of this Mediterranean-style house was
redesigned. Stucco retaining walls, right, create a flat planting area and a
sense of separation from the sidewalk. Tile paves the driveway and paths,
and a strip of blue tile indicates a step. A new garden wall, above left, forms
an interior court. An olive tree and spiky phormium in pots add drama at
the gate. In the court, above right, bougainvillea clambers on the tower.

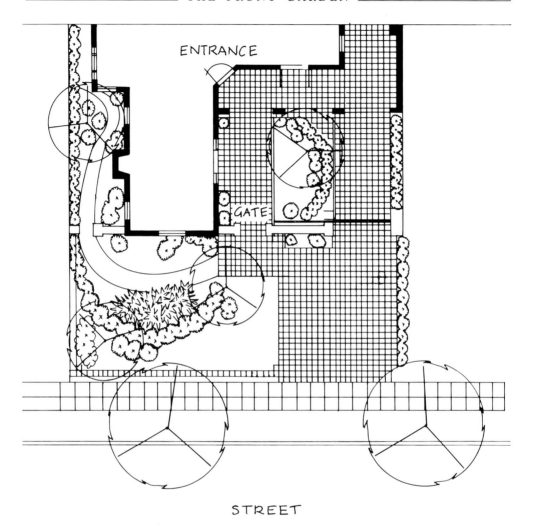

ENTRANCE

GATE

STREET

*The new design for the front property provides garden views from all sides of the
living room ell. A wall encloses the entrance.*

mine's dark glossy green leaves reflect light like mirrors, says Fletcher.

The garden outside the front window is enclosed by a semicircular hedge of *Pittosporum tobira,* which cuts off the view of the window from the street. Blue agapanthus fills a bed in front of the hedge, and a marble font filled with water in the center of the garden seems to float among the tall leaves. Olive trees at each end of the rectangular garden provide vertical accents and additional privacy from the street.

The third garden seen from the living room is the entrance courtyard, visible through French doors. An olive tree, pittosporum hedge, and jasmine groundcover, theme plants of the property, also grow here. Bright seasonal flowers such as orange poppies, lavender, and an old variety of repeat-blooming bearded iris provide a changing display at this much-used entry.

Interesting foliage is one of Fletcher's favorite concerns. The plants for this project were chosen for their ability to withstand drought and for their leaf colors; silvery gray, shiny, reflective dark green, and wine red leaves are his favorites. He chooses olives for their silver leaves, which move in the breeze. *Phormium tenax* 'Bronze Baby', the bronze form of New Zealand flax, is repeated in pots. The tall spikes of phormium are accents among the rounded green and gray shapes of other plants.

The perimeter of the property is hedged with podocarpus, favored for its small, evergreen foliage. In two of the gardens pittosporum provides a backdrop for flowering plants and blocks views from the street. The shiny, thick leaves, curled under at the edges, are arranged on their stems in layered patterns, and create an architectural effect year-round.

Robert Fletcher's design for this small garden demonstrates how structure, pattern, and repetition can divide a property into several individual areas, making it more interesting than it would have been if left as one open space. The walls and hedges create garden rooms with individual personalities and ensure privacy. Tile paving provides structure by delineating pedestrian areas and imposing a strong grid pattern on the ground. Irregular patterns are made by the shadows cast by trees on the paving and walls.

Repetition of materials—stucco for the house and garden walls, tile for roofing and paving—as well as the repetition of plants throughout the garden, unifies the property. The several individual gardens add up to a coherent whole, enriched by detail, planning, and imaginative use of plants.

A MODERN HOUSE
ON A CONNECTICUT HILLTOP

❧

Lester Collins, landscape architect;
William H. Grover, architect

A modern house built of traditional cedar shingles sits on a hilltop, looking into pine and maple woods. The setting is a two-acre site on typically rugged Connecticut land. From the house and entrance area the land falls away to a trout stream rushing over boulders. Large rocks protruding from the ground create natural sculpture throughout the property.

Siting the house took careful study. Architect William Grover and landscape architect Lester Collins scouted the land together to find the ideal spot for the house, leaving the most beautiful existing features of the property intact. They determined that the stream

A lattice-topped fence separates the entrance garden from the parking court.

and pine woods at the low end of the property should stay pristine. The house was set fairly high up where it would be in the open and get light all day.

As Grover describes it, Collins's process of landscaping is subtractive as opposed to additive. He studies a site to discover its strong points, then cleans up, strengthens, and refines the natural features. The essence of each naturally occurring picture is emphasized by eliminating distractions. For instance, brush hiding an interesting rock formation would be removed. Collins repeated the patterns of the existing stone, wood, evergreens, and euonymus to make the landscape picture stronger. He added trees and shrubs where necessary to block the view of a distant house or to enlarge an existing grove of plants. To the casual observer, it looks as though nature has been left undisturbed.

The space for the house and its entrance court was carved out of the hillside. An arriving visitor has little sense of the dramatic views to be seen from the hilltop and the house. The house and its approach were designed to be a series of connected experiences, revealed one at a time. The drive,

hemmed in by shrubby trees, leads to an entrance court enclosed by the house and fences. A smaller court encloses the front door. Then, as you walk through the house, the view over the property is seen through large windows. Finally, a path takes you down the hill to the trout stream, viewed from a gazebo hidden in pine trees.

The arrival area is enclosed by walls, trees, shrubs, boulders, and even stacked firewood. A hint of the Japanese sensibility, which brings together various elements of nature, is at work here. Just as a Japanese garden incorporates rocks, plants, and bamboo to represent the essence of nature, Collins has used wood and rocks, the essence of the Connecticut woods, as both sculpture and structure in the courtyard. A loose pile of boulders on one side of the court acts as an informal retaining wall for the hillside rising above. A 100-foot-long stack of firewood creates a low wall on the far side of the court, making a regular yet irregular pattern, rigid but varied.

The approach to the property is up a steep road shared by several houses. From the road you turn onto a driveway lined with six pollarded weeping

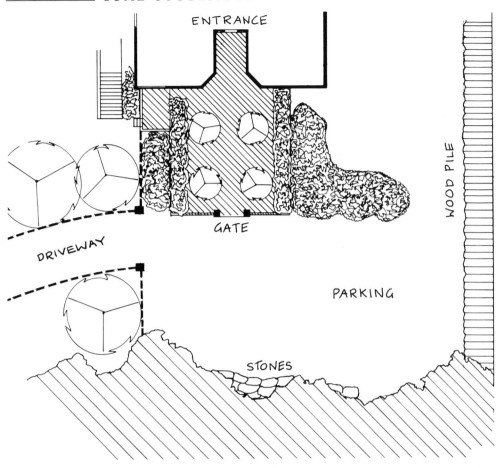

Boulders, a woodpile, and the house define the boundaries of the parking court.

willows *(Salix babylonica)*. Pollarding, a method of severely pruning the tops of trees, has two purposes in this situation. First, it forces branches to sprout on the trunk, making a bushy tree, and second, it makes the brittle willows more compact and less prone to shattering. Willows were used here and in several other spots on the property for their habit of leafing out early in the spring and holding their leaves until late in the fall.

The bushy willows obscure the view of the parking court. To reach it, you drive past the gateposts of a 6-foot-high shingle wall topped with lattice in an open, contemporary pattern. To the left and right of the entrance, the fence

Fences organize space at the entrance to a hilltop house. The enclosed garden, above left, within the parking court. The front door, below left, gives no hint of the views beyond. The driveway, top, passes through dramatic posts. The woodpile, above, forms a wall of the parking area.

steps down in height. The clients who commissioned the house requested that the lattice-topped shingle walls they loved and admired from summers spent on Nantucket be incorporated into the house and property design. Lattice also covers the inside of the walls, making geometric patterns and shadows and providing a structure for ivy to climb on.

From the parking court, paved in crushed stone, the house is on the left. The garage doors cannot be seen. "You should try to arrange it so that you never see garage doors from the approach," says Grover. The garage is on the far side of the house, well hidden from view.

The wall of stacked firewood is on the far side of the court. In the winter, as the wood is used in the fireplaces indoors, the wall shrinks. When it is time to get a new load, the wood is neatly stacked again, with the ends facing the court. The firewood wall constantly expands and contracts. And the person taking the wood into the house gets to decide whether to keep the line as regular as possible by taking pieces from all along the top, or whether to make some sections lower than others

by taking more wood from one area.

A lattice-topped shingle wall also encloses the area at the front door. Here the mood is one of intimacy and expectation. The small court functions as the anteroom of the house, and the solid front door reveals nothing of what lies inside. The court is paved with flagstones with spaces left open for planting. Four Japanese tree lilacs (*Syringa amurensis* var. *japonica*) in the corners have large panicles of fragrant white blossoms in June. Unlike the common shrub lilac, tree lilacs have a single trunk. White clematis, mixed with ivy, twines around the trellis on the inside of the wall.

A collaboration like that between architect William Grover and landscape architect Lester Collins happens seldom. Too often landscaping is an afterthought. The definition of purpose here resulted in a practical and pleasing landscape. Cars have adequate room but can easily be put out of sight. The house entrance is its own enclosed world, and plantings enhance the existing vegetation. The approach to this house is a cerebral study in function and aesthetics, an attractive and appropriate design.

A JAPANESE COURTYARD GARDEN

✗

Design by Michael Glassman,
Environmental Creations, Inc.

A Japanese-style entrance courtyard seemed the inevitable choice for
this low-slung, modern house in California. The small scale, simplicity of
design, and deep roof overhang of the
house, built ten years ago by an architect who drew inspiration from Japan,
suggested an oriental treatment for the
courtyard. The house is U-shaped, with
the entrance at the opening of the U.
The 20-by-40-foot space in the center
was turned into a rock-edged pond
crossed by large stepping stones. The
sound of water trickling over stone creates a contemplative mood, and a few
shrubs and trees add sculptural elements.

Michael Glassman likes designing
Japanese-inspired gardens, particularly
for small spaces. "You can do a lot in a
small space," he says. "It is quiet and

peaceful, a little piece of Shangri-la.
And from a practical point of view, it
is organized and reduces the amount
of clutter." In using elements found
in Japanese gardens—wood, rocks,
water—and plants such as mugo pine
(*Pinus mugo*) and Japanese maple,
(*Acer palmatum*), the American homeowner is borrowing the simplified aesthetic, not the symbolic significance, of
the Japanese garden.

Glassman closed the open side of the
court with a fence built of alternating
narrow and wide vertical boards spaced
several inches apart to create a pattern
of thin and thick, light and dark spaces.
An imposing gate adds a sense of au-
thority and security, enhanced by a
roof extending across the width of the
court. The entrance roof, of the same
material and the same height as the
roof of the house, appears to be an extension of it. The Japanese theme is introduced outside the fence, with
plantings of mugo pines and Japanese
maples flanking the gate, a stone lan-
tern, and large, washed river rocks edging the entrance path of 3-by-10-foot
concrete pads.

The irregular pond is edged with Ne-
vada moss flagstone of varying sizes.

A dramatic approach to the house, right, is over
a pond in a Japanese-style courtyard. The
entrance gate and roof, top, as seen from the
house. Stone lanterns, rock paving, and a mugo
pine set the scene, above, for the entrance to the
Japanese courtyard.

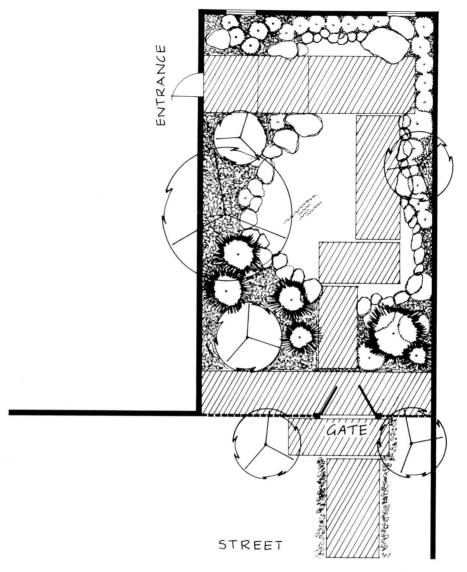

ENTRANCE

GATE

STREET

The house surrounds the entry court and pond.

The pond itself is only 12 inches deep because the building code requires a protective railing along the path by deeper water. Wanting to keep the path open, Glassman decided to build a shallow pond of concrete, coated with black plaster to disguise the bottom and make it appear deeper. The water is recirculated and filtered, and chlorine is used to keep it clear. The water reflects the sky, lightening the garden in the daytime, and at night becoming a bottomless lake.

To reach the front door, one crosses the lake on rectangular poured concrete pads, 3 feet wide by 10 feet long, placed in an alternating vertical and horizontal pattern. Separated by 3-inch spaces, they appear to float on the surface of the water. Their surface of black and white gravel gives them a "contemporary, clean, architectural contrast to the rest of the garden," says Glassman.

The sounds and distractions of the outside world are shut out from this self-contained garden, whose tranquil mood is heightened by the sound of water splashing over stones into the pond. The water trickle is just outside the door, and its soothing sound can be heard inside the house.

In a small garden details are important because every element of the composition is clearly seen. The placement of each plant, the arrangement of the stones, the line of the path—all take on extra significance in an intimate space. One of the most important details in this garden is the variety of textures.

The water is smooth and shiny, the path both pebbled and sharp-edged, large rocks are rough with an overlay of soft moss, and the 6- to 8-inch stones behind the shoreline rocks are large and smooth. Plants provide their own textures.

The plant list is spare and uses several that are found in Japanese gardens. Pines, both low mugos and taller black pines *(Pinus thunbergiana),* provide heft and spiky textures. One large oak towers over the area, creating a pool of shade. Several Japanese maples provide medium-sized plants with fine-textured leaves. A red-leafed variety, one of the few bits of color in the garden other than greens, grays, and browns, stands out like a beacon. Ferns, liriope, and fortnight lily *(Dietes vegeta)* fill in some of the narrow margins of the garden. Groundcovers include baby's tears *(Soleirolia soleirolii)* and blue star creeper *(Laurentia fluviatilis).*

The self-contained Japanese garden puts together pieces of the landscape in a reduced scale to remind us of our connection to nature. It integrates house and environment, with the man-made garden acting as a link between the house and nature.

A WOODLAND ENTRANCE

Design by Craig Bergmann
Landscape Design, Inc.

ROLLING hills and rocky ravines covered by maple woods are characteristic of the landscape in Highland Park in suburban Chicago. When called in to refine a wooded two-acre site in this area, landscape designer Craig Bergmann enhanced the existing woodland to create a private and beautiful approach and entrance to a 1920s Arts and Crafts–style house situated in the center of the property. The landscape design was inspired by the philosophy of Jens Jensen, an influential landscape architect active in the Chicago area at the turn of the century, who advocated the use of indigenous plants to create regional landscapes.

Daffodils and vinca under oak trees brighten a woodland driveway in early spring.

Bergmann added sumac, amelanchier, and hemlocks to the woods, as well as profuse plantings of bulbs, ferns, and rhododendrons under the trees.

The driveway passes through groups of maple trees, which cast dappled light over the understory plantings. Hemlocks planted in groups serve as a privacy buffer and provide touches of green among the tan trunks of the maple trees in winter. Bergmann says his intention was to evoke a sense of traveling back in time as the visitor progresses from the busy street and through the rich wooded tapestry, with the old maple trees harking back to a time when the landscape was untouched.

The woods are laced with walking paths and "council rings," intimate areas cleared for sitting and contemplation. In keeping with the woodland spirit, log benches and tree stumps are artfully placed for seating, and railings made of tree branches provide barriers where the ravine drops away.

The driveway, bordered on both sides by maples and wildflowers, makes a large loop at the entrance to the house. An island planted with hemlocks in the center of the loop, opposite the front door, creates an additional visual buffer from the road. The house, securely tucked away in the woods, is a quiet retreat from the traffic and noise outside. One major consideration in this project was the surface of the drive. When Bergmann was called in, the driveway was gravel, a discreet and suitable look for this forested location. However, the clients, new owners of this property, wanted a durable finish that could be plowed easily in Chicago's long, snowy winters. For practicality, blacktop was put down. To soften the impact of the hard new surface in the midst of such a romantic wooded setting, bricks were extended out from the entrance path into the blacktop surface, making it appear that remnants of an old drive had been incorporated into the new one.

The house entrance is also in the romantic mood. Its wings reach out toward the drive, creating a small courtyard, which has been turned into an intimate garden. There are two entrances to the house from this court, and the path branches off in irregular lines to these doors. The paths and the three façades of the house make a solid backdrop for the flowing shapes of the

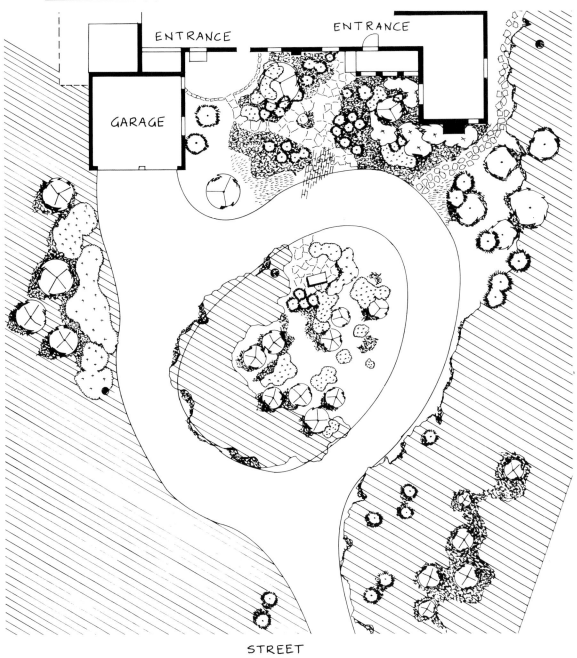

ENTRANCE

ENTRANCE

GARAGE

STREET

The oval garden in the center of the driveway provides privacy and planting beds.

The entrance beds in two seasons. Roses, astilbe, lilies, and ferns, above, brighten the entrance in summer. Bricks extend into the driveway from the path. Chrysanthemums and the orange foliage of amelanchier and sumac announce the fall season, right.

plants and paths. The entrance path echoes the effect of the brick and black-top driveway by mixing areas of flag-stone with seemingly random areas of old brick. There is a hint of antiquity, suggesting that a new stone path was laid over and around an old brick path.

Plants in the entrance garden include woodsy shrubs such as aronia, amelanchier, blueberry, and alder, as well as more refined azaleas. Inkberry and boxwood are dense and green during the cheerless days of winter. Clumps of ferns, hostas, and daylilies soften the twiggy bases of the shrubs, and small spring bulbs grow through areas of groundcover, including euonymus,

vinca, and liriope. A corner of the garden under an old pear tree is devoted to perennials. As one moves away from the house, the plantings become more woodsy, with *Phlox divaricata* planted in drifts under sumacs and gray-green-needled eastern white pines.

The woodland entrance has been designed to provide a protected setting and approach for a suburban house. The maples and hemlocks between the house and road create a feeling of solitude, a sense of remoteness from neighbors and traffic; this tranquil mood is retained throughout the year. Carefully considered plantings of deciduous perennials and wildflowers add seasonal excitement, with colorful flowers and foliage with textural variety from May through November. In winter, when snow blankets the ground, the stark trunks of trees and the deep green needles of the evergreens dress up the woodsy landscape.

BIBLIOGRAPHY

Balmori, D., D. McGuire, and E. McPeck. *Beatrix Farrand's American Landscapes.* Millwood, N.Y.: Sagapress, 1985.

Church, T. *Gardens Are for People.* New York: McGraw Hill, 1983.

Creasy, Rosalind. *The Complete Book of Edible Landscaping.* San Francisco: Sierra Club Books, 1982.

Earle, A. M. *Old Time Gardens.* New York: Macmillan, 1901.

Eckbo, G. *The Art of Home Landscaping.* New York: F. W. Dodge, 1956.

Fogle, D., C. Mahan, and C. Weeks. *Clues to American Garden Styles.* Washington, D.C.: Starrhill Press, 1987.

Gothein, M. L. *A History of Garden Art.* New York: Hacker Art Books, 1966.

Hedrick, U. P. *A History of Horticulture in America to 1860.* New York: Oxford University Press, 1950.

Jekyll, G., and L. Weaver. *Gardens for Small Country Houses.* 1912. Reprint, London: Antique Collectors' Club, 1981.

Jellicoe, G., S. Jellicoe, P. Goode, and M. Lancaster. *The Oxford Companion to Gardens.* New York: Oxford University Press, 1986.

Johnson, H. *The Principles of Gardening.* New York: Simon and Schuster, 1984.

Lacy, A., ed. *The American Gardener.* New York: Farrar, Straus & Giroux, 1988.

Leighton, A. *American Gardens in the Eighteenth Century.* Amherst, Mass.: University of Massachusetts Press, 1986.

McGuire, D. K. *Gardens of America.* Charlottesville, Va.: Thomasson-Grant, 1989.

Ortloff, H. S., and H. Raymore. *The Book of Landscape Design.* New York: Barrows, 1959.

Page, R. *The Education of a Gardener.* New York: Random House, 1983.

Thacker, C. *The History of Gardens.* Berkeley: University of California Press, 1979.

Verey, R. *The Garden in Winter.* Boston: Little, Brown, 1988.

Wilder, L. B. *My Garden.* New York: Doubleday, Page, 1920.

ILLUSTRATION CREDITS

PHOTO CREDITS

Atlanta Historical Society 18(2)

Suzanne Bales for W. Atlee Burpee & Co. 38–39, 74(top), 75(top), 102(2)

Liz Ball 2–3, 31, 34, 50(top), 62(top), 103(top)

Karen Balogh 66

Margaret Bowditch 67(right)

Judith Bromley for Craig Bergmann Landscape Design 174–175, 178, 179

Child Associates: Doug Reed 150; Alan Ward 150–151, 154–155, 155

Langdon Clay for Cooper, Robertson & Partners 59(top)

Lucy Coggin for Historic Annapolis 23

Rosalind Creasy 75(bottom), 122, 142–143, 143, 146, 147, endpapers

Hugh and Mary Palmer Dargan, ASLA, Charleston, S.C.: Carola Kittredge-Lott 87(top), 110; Alexander L. Wallace 86(bottom), 110–111

Catherine Davis 139(top)

Environmental Creations, Inc. 170(2), 170–171

Derek Fell 30(top), 38(bottom), 51

Robert M. Fletcher 158(2), 159

Balthazar Korab 11, 22–23, 27, 42(bottom), 43(bottom), 62(bottom), 86(top), 99

Robert Kourik 30(bottom), 38(top)

Scott G. Kunst 14, 70(top), 103(bottom)

Jerry Lee for Landscape Design Associates 114–115

Robert Levin for Centerbrook Architects and Planners 162–163, 166(2), 167(2)

Peter Loewer 95(2)

Carola Kittredge-Lott 70(bottom)

Charles Mann 59(bottom), 67(left), 78(bottom), 94

Tom Mannion 138, 139(bottom)

Elizabeth P. McLean 26(bottom)

W. Scott Mitchell 26(top), 42(top), 106, 107

Maggie Oster 79

Jerry Pavia 54, 82, 90, 91, 118(top), 119, 127(top), 134(bottom), 135

Joanne Pavia 63, 98, 126–127, 127(bottom), 130–131, 134(top)

Lanny Provo 115

Allen Rokach for W. Atlee Burpee & Co. 43(top)

Lauren Springer 6

Strawbery Banke 8–9

George Taloumis 19, 46–47, 70–71, 78(top), 87(bottom)

Walpole Woodworkers 50(bottom), 58

Alan Ward 118(bottom)

DRAWING CREDITS

Keva Miles 64, 65, 68, 76, 85, 101, 116

Ronan O'Sullivan 61, 69, 73, 89

Linda Winters 125, 133, 137, 145, 149, 153, 160, 165, 172, 177

ACKNOWLEDGMENTS

THE creation of a book involves many people who support and encourage the author. I have two editors to thank for their help: Sarah Kirshner, who helped me organize and start writing, and Anne Halpin, who edited the finished product. Picture editor Ellie Watson gathered wonderful illustrations and was gracious about my numerous inquiries about photos. Kathleen Westray did a lovely job designing the book.

Gardening friends Pamela Lord, Lynden Miller, and Mike Graham have generously shared their knowledge and understanding of gardens and plants over the years. My colleague Eileen Imber gave me time to write. And friends and clients believed in my ability to create gardens, making it possible for me to practice my profession as a garden designer. The support of Annie, Eric, and Jay Gleacher was essential in getting started.

My sister Nancy Newhouse, a magazine and newspaper editor, gets special thanks for encouraging me to become a writer. She gave me the opportunity to write articles before garden design became my full-time profession. Without those earlier efforts I would not have had the confidence to attempt a book. Most of all, I am grateful to my sons, Joshua and Ethan, and my husband, Tony, who have been patient, supportive, and understanding. This book was possible because of their faith and generosity.

My thanks to all the people at Running Heads who made this book possible, including Marta Hallett, Ellen Milionis, Linda Winters, Lindsey Crittenden, and Charles de Kay.

Many people were generous with suggestions and time, including Lee Adler, Savannah, Georgia; Susanne Bales, W. Atlee Burpee & Co., Warminster, Pennsylvania; Lynn Batdorf, U.S. National Arboretum, Washington, D.C.; Patrick Chasse, Northeast Harbor, Maine; Leslie Close, New York; Jennie and Peter Cure, Phoenix; Robert DePrisco, New York; Robert Ermerins of Robert A. M. Stern Architects, New York; Rudy Favretti, Storrs, Connecticut; Christopher C. Freidrichs, New Orleans; Frank and Rick of the F.V.R. Corporation, Bridgehampton, New

York; Ryan Gainey, Atlanta; Isabelle Green, Santa Barbara; Richard Haag, Seattle; Bruce Kelly of Kelly Varnell Landscape Architects, New York; Carola Lott, Millbrook, New York; Ann Masaury, Strawbery Banke Museum, Portsmouth, New Hampshire; Brian Murphy, B.A.M. Construction and Design, Santa Monica; Mary O'Rourke, Centerbrook Architects, Essex, Connecticut; Charlotte Peters and Anita Phillipsborn, Evanston, Illinois; Colvin Randall, Longwood Gardens, Kennet Square, Pennsylvania; Shirley Reese, Green Animals, Portsmouth, Rhode Island; Shirley F. Reiss, The Preservation Society of Newport County, Newport, Rhode Island; Jaquelin Robertson of Cooper, Robertson and Partners, New York; Ann Strachan, New Orleans; Alta Tingle, The Gardener, Berkeley; Greg Trutza, New Directions in Landscape Architecture, Phoenix; James van Sweden, Oehme van Sweden Associates, Washington, D.C.; Rick William, San Francisco; Elisabeth Woodburn, Booknoll Farm, Hopewell, New Jersey.

M.R.S.

❧ ❧ ❧ ❧ ❧ ❧ ❧ ❧ ❧

SOURCES

This list includes those architects, landscape architects, and garden designers whose work is featured in this book.

Craig Bergman Landscape Design
1924 Lake Avenue
Wilmette, IL 60091

Centerbrook Architects
P.O. Box 955
Essex, CT 06426

Child Associates
26 Church Street
Cambridge, MA 02138

Cooper, Robertson & Partners
311 West 43 Street
New York, NY 10036

Rosalind Creasy
146 Lockhart Lane
Los Altos, CA 94022

Hugh Dargan Associates
P.O. Box 357
Charleston, SC 29402

Environmental Creations, Inc.
Michael Glassman
1483 Shore Street
Sacramento, CA 95691

Robert M. Fletcher Landscape Design
1000 Monument Street
Pacific Palisades, CA 90272

Ryan Gainey
The Connoisseur's Garden
3165 E. Shadowlawn Ave N.E.
Altanta, GA 30305

William Gleckman
310 East 69 Street
New York, NY 10021

Hugh Newall Jacobson
2529 P Street, N.W.
Washington, D.C. 20007

LDA Architects
Jerry Lee
1108-A Bryant Street
San Francisco, CA 94115

Schwartz, Smith, Meyer Landscape
  Architects, Inc.
Martha Schwartz
2222 Bush Street
San Francisco, CA 94115

Oehme, vanSweden Associates
800 G Street
Washington, D.C. 20003

Robert A. M. Stern Architects
211 West 61 Street
New York, NY 10023

Larry Underhills
3580 Southwest Burlwood
Beaverton, OR 97005

Page numbers of illustrations are in italics

perennial, 130, *130–31*, 132–34, *134,*
135
sculpture, *118, 119,* 120–21
swimming pool in, 109, 112–13, *114–*
15, 117
tennis court in, 113, 116–17
urban, 148–49, *150–51,* 152–53, *154–*
55, 155
vegetable, *75,* 80, 85, 88, *122,* 141, *142–*
43, 143–47, *146,* 147
woodland, 149, 174, *174–75,* 176–79,
178, 179
See also Foundation planting
Front garden, designing, 35–53
budget in, 53
drawings in, 48, 52–53
functional needs and, 36–37
integration with neigborhood, 37, 40
model building in, 52
professional input in, 48–49, 52, 53
reasons for, 35–36
regulations/ordinances in, 40
sources of ideas, 47–48
See also Driveway; Garage; Parking area;
Paths; Service buildings; Style,
selecting
Front garden, history of, 15–33
California school, 32–33
colonial dooryard, 16–17, *19*
cottage, *14,* 17, *18,* 20
development of lawns, 28–29
eighteenth-century pleasure, 20–21,
22–23, 24
foundation planting in, 27, 29, *30,* 32
reaction against lawn, 32
Spanish courtyard, 24–25, *26*

synthesis in, 33
Victorian, 25, *26, 27, 28,* 29

G
Gainey, Ryan, 74, 86
Garage, 56, 61
eliminating, 68
masked by plantings, *62, 63,* 64
moving entrance, 68, 125, 128, 168
See also Parking area
Garden designer, 48–49, 52, 53
Gardenesque style, 25, 28
Garden Gate Landscaping, Inc., 136
Gardens for Small Country Houses (Jekyll),
40–41
Gardens of America (McGuire), 24
Gardens of the Governor's Palace,
Williamsburg (Shurcliff), 21
Gates, 45, *58, 59, 82, 150*
Geometric garden, 20, 21
Geraniums, *62,* 77
perennial, 132
Ginger, European (*Asarum europaeum*),
148
Glassman, Michael, 169, 172–73
Gleckman, William, 112
Grapevine, 66
Grass(es), 57, 89, 92–93, *95,* 129, 136–
38, *138, 139,* 140
See also Lawn
Gravel
colored, 120
driveway, 60
Greenfield Village, Michigan, *14,* 22–23
Grover, William H., 163, 164, 168

M
McGuire, Diane Kostial, 24
Magnolia, 23
    star *(Magnolia tomentosa)*, 152, *155*
Mannion, Tom, 136–37, 140
Maple, 176
    Japanese *(Acer palmatum)*, 121, 149,
        169, 173
    Norway, 136
Marguerites, 144
Marigolds, 17, *142*
Masury, Ann, 105
Meadow, 88–89, 92
Meconopsis cambrica, 132
Miscanthus, 93, *95*
    M. sinensis 'Gracillimus', 93
Montbretia, 144
Morey, Clayton, 125, 128
Morning glories, *67*, 77
Morris, Hilda, 121
Mountain laurel *(Kalmia latifolia)*, 149,
    152
Mount Vernon, Virginia, 21, 24
Mugo pine *(Pinus mugo)*, 169, 173
Myosotis scorpioides, 132, 134

N
Naturalistic style, 24, 25

O
Oehme, van Sweden and Associates, 92,
    140
Old Time Gardens (Earle), 20, 28–29
Oleander, 101

Orchard, 89, 92
Osmanthus, 101

P
Paca (William) House, Annapolis, Md.,
    21, 23
Pachysandra, *119*, 121
Panicum virgatum, 93
Pansies, 62
Parking area, 37, 56, 148, 168
    enclosure as, 117
    masked by plantings, 64–65, 67
    separation of, *59*, 72, 128
    surface of, 65, 67, 128
    turning Y, 64
    See also Driveway; Garage
Paths, *122*, 137, 140, *142*, 143, *150–51*,
    152, *158*
    function of, 72
    layout of, 72–73
    secondary, 76, 128
    surface of, *51*, *54*, *70–71*, 72, 73, 76,
        178
    transition and, 52, 72
Pennisetum, 95
    P. alopecuroides, 93
Peonies, 20, 29, 129
Perennial garden, 130, *130–31*, 132–34,
    134, *135*
Pergola, *66*, *122*
Perilla, *142*
Periwinkle *(Vinca minor)*, 152, *174–75*,
    179
Phalaris canariensis, 129
Phlox, 20, 43
    divaricata, 179